اردو
แบบ
Svenska
Dansk
Tiếng Việt
Norsk Bokmål
Polski
Suomi
Bahasa
Indonesia
תיﬧבﬠ
Ελληνικά
Română
Magyar
Čeština
Català
Slovenčina
Український
Hrvatski
Bahasa Melayu
हिन्दी

English
Français
Deutsch
简体中文
中國傳統的
日本語
Español
Русский
Português
Italiano
한국인
Türkçe
Nederlands

"More people in the world have access to a mobile phone than a toilet."

quote from U.N. report

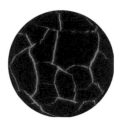

Select Your Country or Region

Afghanistan
Albania
Algeria
Andorra
Angola
Antigua and Barbuda
Argentina
Armenia
Australia
Austria
Azerbaijan

Bahamas
Bahrain
Bangladesh
Barbados
Belarus
Belgium
Belize
Benin
Bhutan
Bolivia
Bosnia and Herzegovina

Botswana
Brazil
Brunei
Bulgaria
Burkina Faso
Burundi

Cabo Verde
Cambodia
Cameroon
Canada
Central African Republic (CAR)
Chad
Chile
China
Colombia
Comoros
Congo, Democratic Republic of the
Congo, Republic of the Costa Rica
Côte d'Ivoire
Croatia
Cuba
Cyprus
Czechia

D

Denmark
Djibouti
Dominica
Dominican Republic

E

Ecuador
Egypt
El Salvador
Equatorial Guinea
Eritrea
Estonia
Eswatini
Ethiopia

F

Fiji
Finland
France

G

Gabon
Gambia
Georgia
Germany
Ghana
Greece
Grenada
Guatemala
Guinea
Guinea-Bissau
Guyana

H

Haiti
Honduras
Hungary

I

Iceland
India
Indonesia
Iran
Iraq
Ireland
Israel
Italy

J

Jamaica
Japan
Jordan

K

Kazakhstan
Kenya
Kiribati
Kosovo
Kuwait
Kyrgyzstan

L

Laos
Latvia
Lebanon
Lesotho
Liberia
Libya
Liechtenstein
Lithuania
Luxembourg

M

Madagascar
Malawi
Malaysia
Maldives

Mali
Malta
Marshall Islands
Mauritania
Mauritius
Mexico
Micronesia
Moldova
Monaco
Mongolia
Montenegro
Morocco
Mozambique
Myanmar

Namibia
Nauru
Nepal
Netherlands
New Zealand
Nicaragua
Niger
Nigeria
North Korea
North Macedonia
Norway

Oman

Pakistan
Palau
Palestine
Panama
Papua New Guinea
Paraguay
Peru

Philippines
Poland
Portugal

Qatar

Romania
Russia
Rwanda

Saint Kitts and Nevis
Saint Lucia
Saint Vincent and the Grenadines
Samoa
San Marino
Sao Tome and Principe
Saudi Arabia
Senegal
Serbia
Seychelles
Sierra Leone
Singapore
Slovakia
Slovenia
Solomon Islands
Somalia
South Africa
South Korea
South Sudan
Spain
Sri Lanka
Sudan
Suriname
Sweden
Switzerland
Syria

T

Taiwan
Tajikistan
Tanzania
Thailand
Timor-Leste
Togo
Tonga
Trinidad and Tobago
Tunisia
Turkey
Turkmenistan
Tuvalu

U

Uganda
Ukraine
United Arab Emirates (UAE)
United Kingdom (UK)
United States of America (USA)
Uruguay
Uzbekistan

V

Vanuatu
Vatican City (Holy See)
Venezuela
Vietnam

Y

Yemen

Z

Zambia
Zimbabwe

Choose a Wi-Fi Network

Free Internet
LAN-Rover
Chipotle Guest
Unprotected
CeX
disconnected
Malware.exe
Nina
UPC56749301
Wedonthavewifi
Crack Shack
TMNL-6872382
2 Girls 1 Router
Zigg0

Next Nature
Network
DeathStar Guest
No 5G
Room 134's WiFi
DeltaWiPhi
Batlan and Login
Password
Paul 76

Choose Another
Network

It may take a few minutes to activate your book.

BIS Publishers
Borneostraat 80A
1094CP Amsterdam
www.bispublishers.com

Next Nature
Evoluon
Noord Brabantlaan 1A
5652 LA Eindhoven
The Netherlands
www.nextnature.net

SWIPE

Mieke Gerritzen
Ieva Jakusa

Published by
BIS Publishers

It owns your data
It knows your friends
It has your credit cards
It hears your conversations
It follows you everywhere
And you can't go a day
without it.

TABLE OF CONTENTS

"The smartphone today is either a digital workplace or a digital confessional. Every device, and every technique of domination, generates totems that are used for subjugation. This is how domination is strengthened. The smartphone is the cult object of digital domination."

Byung-Chul Han (Korean philosopher)

FOREWORD →

Swipe represents a fleeting touch—or not quite. With Swipe, life flashes, flits and floats by. Swipe brings you information that almost escaped your attention but happened to catch your eye. Swipe represents the information society we live in. Swipe stands for coincidence. Swipe belongs to a time where we see everything in the lives of others and yet remain endlessly in search of ourselves. Swipe is relaxation. Swipe is boredom, but also interest and absorption. Swiping can be done out of love, but also out of hate and aversion. Swiping is what we do en masse, unconsciously, all day long.

The book Swipe doesn't aim to demonstrate that the smartphone is bad for humanity. The smartphone is a means of communication, a bridge through the air between human and society. Through its ever-expanding functionality, it's getting closer and closer to its user, and is already almost a body part, something you can no longer do without. Even if the device isn't literally incorporated into the human body just yet, its impact can already be felt under the skin. Remarkably, constant smartphone use isn't listed so far as a known addiction in the handbook of mental disorders. For that, more research is needed into the specific personality traits of people who simply can't resist the temptation of their phones. But it's easy to imagine we might just as well skip this diagnosis, since what first seemed like a condition has become the norm. Maybe the feeling of indispensability in this case indicates not a disease or addiction, but an evolutionary development. Homo sapiens came into existence through the gradual mutation of ape into human. Do we imagine that change happened without criticism? It's easy to imagine that there were apes who viewed the transformation as unnatural and protested against it. Human reason isn't necessary for such a reaction to arise; instinct suffices to make you resist change.

The transition humanity is currently undergoing is just as radical. The fusion of human and technology has already been going on for some time, under various names; "AI" and "robot" are the best known right now, but how the technological humans 100 years hence will be known is anyone's guess.

The smartphone is a symbol of the current phase in the development of the human species. It holds up a mirror to us and, at the same time, serves as a tool for shaping our image of ourselves and our lives. Identity was once shaped primarily by ancestry and community; in an online society, we create our own stories in an environment of our choice. Or is that just an illusion? Does the device merely allow government and commerce greater influence on our inner selves, limiting freedom of choice to externals, to amusement? Is the smartphone developing as a sense, or as a means of control in the hands of a society that intervenes more extensively in the lives of its citizens than ever before?

SWIPE is critical, looks from the perspective of the user, and seeks the positive effects of smartphone use. In this way, we can develop an understanding of digital self-reflection that goes beyond the selfie. 🙂

Mieke Gerritzen

How this book works ↓

SWIPE is a user-manual experience for smart-phone users, inspired by the good old printed manuals that come with any newly purchased technology. Today, new users are left without a printed companion that helps navigate their phone. SWIPE is here to help. SWIPE transcends the user manual, and offers insights to the often ignored anxieties and excitements that users might have about their most beloved device. Even when there's no wifi.

Swiping through this manual, users will encounter five categories that offer guidance. SURVIVAL speaks about how the smartphone helps users survive, and whether it itself will survive. SENSE OF SELF reflects on how the user's being is constructed by the smartphone, and vice versa. HABITS focuses on the user's daily use of the smartphone, and how its constant presence shapes daily life. RESOURCES speaks about how nature and users give power to the smartphone. And lastly, EXISTENTIAL CRISIS reflects on how the smartphone is used to escape the anxieties of real-life, while it simultaneously creates a world of more abstract questions.

Inspired by the format of Frequently Asked Questions, SWIPE presents questions about the smartphone that users might have (not) frequently asked themselves. In order to reflect the endlessly diverse and dynamic content users daily swipe for on their smartphone, these questions are not followed by single sentences, but by image collections consisting of Internet-found visuals. Contemporary writers and artists will help users embrace their newly acquired knowledge by guiding them through reflective visions of the age of the smartphone. Complemented by thought-provoking concepts and definitions in the Smartphone Glossary, these help users unpack ideas typical for the smartphone-era.

SWIPE invites each user to swipe through this manual like they would on their smartphones, using this manual to turn their uncertainties into excitement, anxieties into clarity, and confrontation into reflection.

Beau Magdelijns and Ieva Jakusa

SURVIVAL

The user existed way before the
smartphone. Once a caveman
using a stone, the user now holds
a phone. The device has made
momentous changes in how the
user navigates life, nature and their
place in history, as it assists the
user in surviving the current era.
In turn, the user helps the smartphone to survive, by using it. But,
the user might one day choose
to carry another tool, if the smartphone itself fails to survive.

1

1.1 Remember the dumb-phone? ↗

figure 1

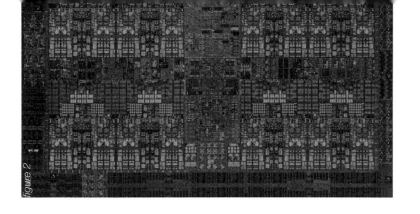

figure 2

figure 3

Repetitive Strain Injury prevention software
"Workrave" *by 2stepsback posted on Donation Coder / 2007 /* Workrave gives a 30-second count-down timer and then locks your input devices so you can see the standard screen, but nothing works. That's a "microbreak" - the default is one every three minutes!! A rest break is about 5 minutes long and can be set at particular intervals. The user can also skip or postpone the break notifications.

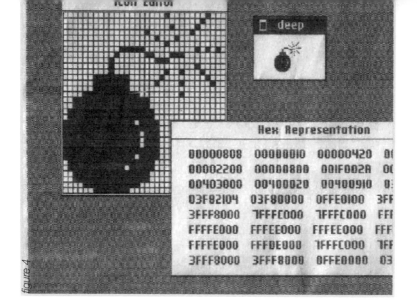

figure 4

Hex Representation

00000808	00000010	00000420	0(
00002200	00000880	001F002A	0(
00403000	00400020	00400910	0:
03F82104	03F80000	0FFE0100	3FF
3FFF8000	7FFFC000	7FFFC000	FFF
FFFFE000	FFFEE000	FFFEE000	FFF
FFFFE000	FFFDE000	7FFFC000	7FF
3FFF8000	3FFF8000	0FFE0000	03

Sketch and code for Apple graphic **"user icon"** *by Susan Kare /* Printed material, dot matrix,17 × 22 cm / 1983 / Kare's aim was to create icons that were distinct, simple but could also call up visual queues of what she wanted them to do.

figure 5

figure 6
Oh, my God, he's online. Can he see me?

1.2 How can I celebrate my addiction? ↗

figure 7

figure 8

30

figure 9

Mixed media scanography on iPhone X 2019
index **"Smart Phone"** by Maggie Cnossen

figure 10

31

NOMOPHOBIA
/ no-mo-foh-bee-uh /
noun

1.1

The fear and anxiety experi-
enced when physically detached from
a smartphone or being detached from
mobile phone connectivity.

↗

TEXTESE

/ tekst-ees /
noun

1.2

A form of typed language used
in text messages, characterized by
the omission of words and the use of
abbreviations, letter/number homo-
phones, and emoticons.

1.3 Can we write history with our smart- phones? ↗

figure 11

↑ *Photography* **"Palestine"** *by Gharabli Ahmad / December 16, 2017 /* A Palestinian woman takes a picture of a member of the Israeli security forces as he takes her picture in a street in Jerusalem.

↑ *Shot from a video by Frazier Darnella / May 25, 2020 / December 16, 2017 /* Derek Chauvin kneeling on George Floyd's neck in Minneapolis.

figure 13

Look at this brave woman who openly asks a Russian soldier: "Why did you come to our country?"

... "put sunflower seeds in their pockets so they grow when they die on Ukrainian land."

Henichesk, a port city along the Sea of Azov in Kherson Oblast of southern Ukraine.

36

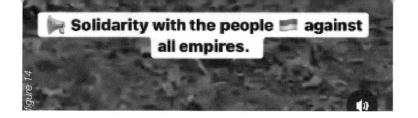

figure 14

Solidarity with the people against
all empires.

figure 15

ME TOO

*Protest Photography by Elvert Barnes / January
20, 2018 /* Baltimore Women's March Gathering
Rally at War Memorial Plaza at 101 North Gay Street in
Baltimore, Maryland.

figure 18

figure 17

Protest Photography by papas_imaculate / July 9, 2022 / Sri Lankan protesters watching their protest in the presidential house.

CLICKTIVISM

/ klik-tuh-viz-uhm /
noun

1.3

The use of the internet to support political or social causes in ways that require minimal effort, for example creating or signing online petitions.

DOOMSCROLLING
/ doom-skroh-ling /
verb

1.3

The practice of obsessively and continually scrolling through news updates using a smartphone, with the expectation that the news will be saddening, disheartening, or depressing.

figure 18

1.4 Is my smart-phone a survival kit? ↗

figure 19

SURVIVAL

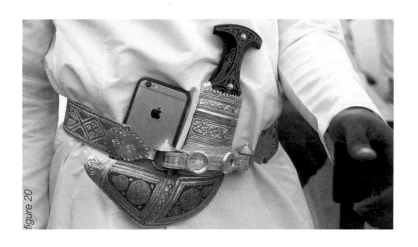
figure 20

 c*****x 👍 ⋯

★☆☆☆☆

玻璃螢幕跟金屬接縫那邊會割手，你他媽跟我說這是正常現象？

figure 21

2021-06-04 23:28

figure 22

figure 23

4.4

SMARTPHONE STALKING
/ smahrt-fohn staw-king /
verb

1.4

The practice of stalking by downloading spyware applications on one's smartphone that allow the stalker to track someone's device activity.

1.5 Technology has evolved, but has my brain?

figure 24

↑ *Installation* **"txt me when u get here"** *by James Bayard* / Nylon 10' x 19' 2010 / The flag presides over a domain which has dual meaning with the virtual space of the Internet, as well as the physical geography of the space in which it is shown.

People who liked this also liked...

Mount Cook
1323 km South

One Tree Hill
401 km North East

Uluru
4291 km North West

↑ *Temporary Installation* **"Mountain"** *by Scott Kelly and Ben Polkinghorne* / New Zealand. 2016 / As the online world makes its way more and more into our offline world, Ben and Scott wanted to make people question how the decisions are made. And how much online algorithms can influence that decision making.

Woman Follows GPS, Drives Car Into Canada's Georgian Bay

figure 29
© Andrea Vincze

figure 30

1.6 Is there such a thing as "pho-nosynthesis"? ↗

figure 31

50

figure 32

figure 33

Performance **"Phonosynthesis"** *by Sophiyah E. with Detroit Bureau of Sound, and 3k /* Cranbrook Art Museum, 2022 /

PHONOSYNTHESIS

/ fohn-uh-sin-thuh-sis /

verb

1.6

A future process in which plants take in carbon dioxide (CO_2) and water (H_2O) from the air and soil, and turn it into oxygen not by sunlight, but by using light from a phone screen.

↗

figure 34

1.7 What does my phone's future look like?

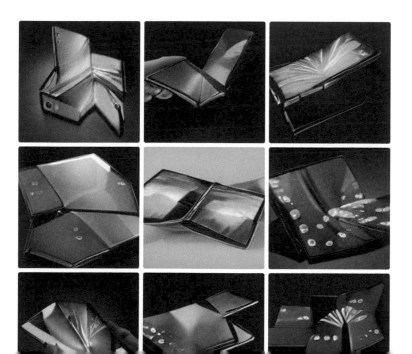

figure 35-44

↑ *AI generated image* **"foldable futuristic smart-phone"** *algorithm by Boris Dayma* / 2022 /

figure 45

figure 46

figure 47

↑ *Calm User Interface* **"Envelope"** *by Special Projects Studio* / 2020 / One envelope turns your phone into a very basic device which can only make and receive calls, while the other turns your phone into a photo and video camera with no screen, helping you focus on what's in front of you.

figure 48

1.8 **Will smart-phones ever go extinct?**

figure 49

figure 50

figure 51

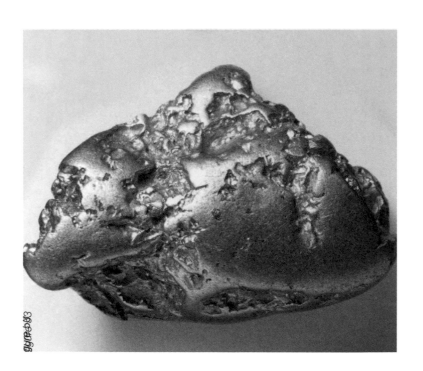

figure 53

figure 52

figure 54

Essay by
Henk Oosterling

The Index of Literacy

How does the index finger move over the touchscreen? Is his function only to cancel or like? Or does that finger also point to the in between space of doubt? A light touch to the right, or back and then to the left. Can you see it clearly or do you spread your fingertips apart to get a closer look at the image? Is it indexical hesitation or reconsideration? Long ago, reading and writing was inspired by the proportions of the index finger with its one long and two short finger cages. Dáktylo - Greek for 'finger' - denoted a 'foot' in poetic meter, consisting of a long syllable followed by two short syllables.

Visualize Brad Pitt playing Achilles in Troy (2004). The film is based on Homer's Iliad, one of the sources of Western civilization. Homer's verses were written in hexameters, each consisting of six dactyls. At that time, rhapsodes, who roamed from one village to another, recited these elaborate verses by heart. They were able to remember these thanks to the hexametric rhythm. Reading and writing texts is still basic in school education. But there is also a frantic search for systems in which and with which we can read and understand images, because nowadays most communication is image-related. Recent neuroscience research from MIT concluded that the brain can identify images that are perceived in just 13 milliseconds.

The index finger connects mind and matter. It has always been an exclusive medium for referring to the origin and destiny of man, albeit from different angles and in different directions. The prophet Moses, carrying the clay tablets with the Ten Commandments, points straight up. In a famous Zen anecdote, Buddha's illuminated index finger points diagonally to the moon. Michelangelo's creation fresco on the ceiling of the Vatican's Sistine Chapel shows Adam and God reaching out horizontally. And after God's demise in the 19th century, modern individuals point towards a utopian "dot on the horizon." Yet no one has ever touched the real thing, up there, out there, beyond, and—in modern times—in there, our self-consciousness. There has always been an inter space between the finger and the material world. An in-between space - or an intermediate period - to interpret, reconsider and contemplate.

Digital media, computers, laptops, iPads and smartphones, were once designed to handle communications more efficiently than printed media. But as early as 1964, Marshall McLuhan predicted that the medium would eventually turn into the message. Everything became media. And with digital media, everything became information. We ourselves have become information too. Informing ourselves, we maneuver in between the explorative, liberating use and the oppressive, addictive impact of, for example, the smartphone. That is the inter space in which the index finger sometimes hesitates. At Facebook, Twitter and TikTok, that gap has completely disappeared due to the algorithmic framing and spamming of the same thing.

We now live in the Anthropocene. We have become ambiguous nodes in networks. With the fingers with which a pen used to be dipped in ink, we now swipe on screens, absorbing images that, just like our blood, flow through our bodies as information. How media literate can our index finger become?

SENSE ⊙F SELF

The user is co-evolving with their smartphone. They try to make sense of themselves, by sharing with their phone their deepest fears and longings. The user dresses their smartphone to match their outfit and reflect their style. In turn, the smartphone dresses them, shaping the way the user relates to themselves, co-constructing their online identity, and with that, their real-life sense of self.

2.1 Is my identity made of pixels?

YOU'RE NOT DEEP
YOU'RE NOT AN INTELLECTUAL
YOU'RE NOT AN ARTIST

figure 57

figure 58

figure 59

Virtual Wedding!
.com
s.

figure 60

↑ *A snapshot of* **"the ringbearers delivering the rings through the cloud wedding"** *by Virbela* / 2021 / For their wedding in the metaverse, Dave and Traci Gagnon had avatars created that were based on personal photos and the clothes they wore to their in-person ceremony.

Within a computer program or website, a user is often represented by an abstract icon of a person

figure 62

2.2 Can I use my phone without thumbs? ↗

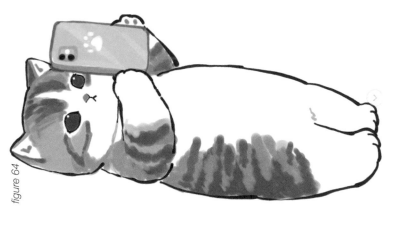

figure 64

figure 65

figure 66

if social media
collapses i will
stand on the street
holding up hand
painted memes

figure 70-74

FAT FINGER
/ fat fing-ger /
noun

2.2

An expression referring to the phenomenon of fingers being "too fat" to accurately depress the keys on the smartphone's screen, often resulting in a typo due to more than one key being pressed at the same time.

↗

figure 75

2.3 What is my taste in phones?

figure 76

25%
Easy Slide

74

A project **"Consumables"** by artist Boo Chapple,
with photography by Bo Wong / 2009 / Consumables is not intended as a serious design proposal.
Instead, Chapple's project plays with the inherent absur-
dity of environmental solutions that rely upon continued,
and unsustainable, levels of consumption.

figure 80

2.4 Is my phone an influencer?

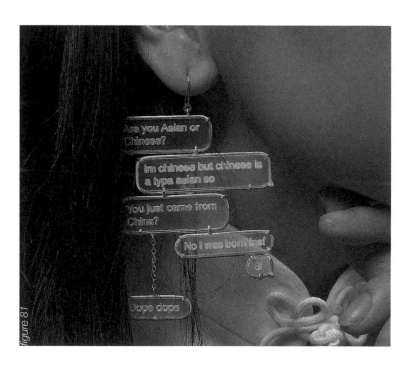

Are you Asian or Chinese?

Im chinese but chinese is a typa asian so

You just came from China?

No I was born insf

Dope dope

figure 81

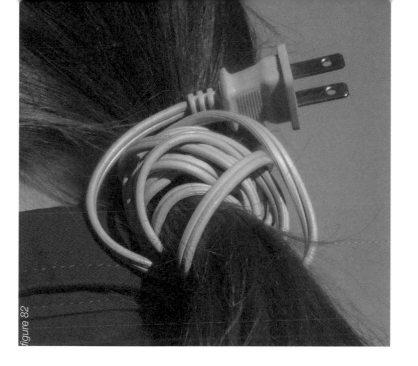
figure 82

figure 83

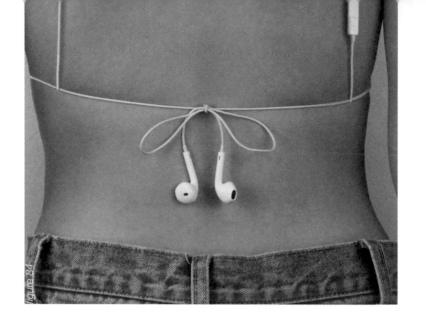

figure 84

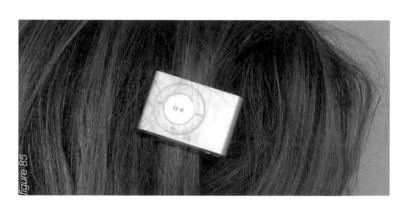

figure 85

78

↑ *Photograph* **"phony heels"** *by Gab Bois*
/ 2021 /

figure 88

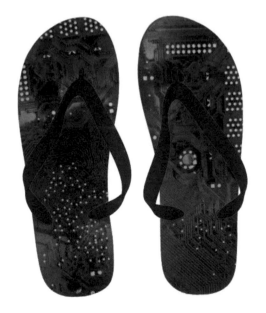

figure 89

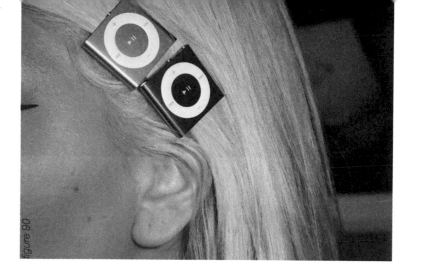
figure 90

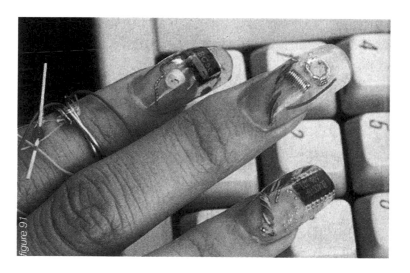
figure 91

figure 92

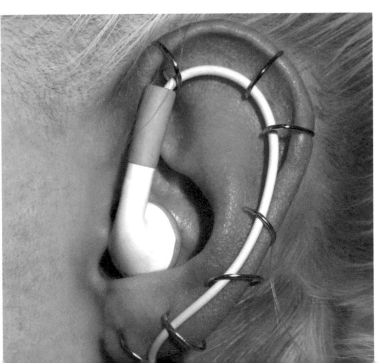

82

2.5 Does my phone colonize my body? ↗

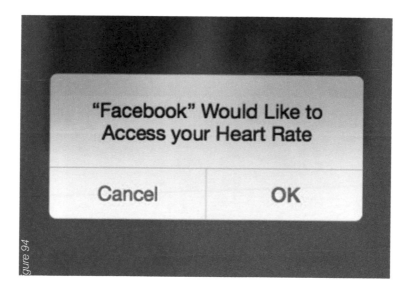

figure 94

"Facebook" Would Like to Access your Heart Rate

Cancel   OK

*Photograph **"Neil Harbisson"** by Cyborg Arts Limited / 2020 / Neil Harbisson is a Catalan-raised, British-born contemporary artist and cyborg activist best known for having an antenna implanted in his skull and for being officially recognised as a cyborg by government.*

figure 97

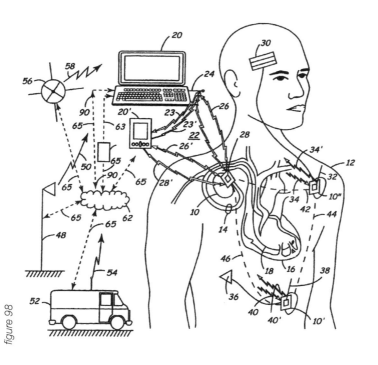

figure 98

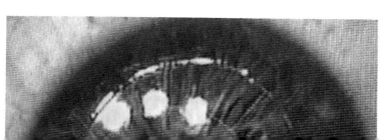

SELF-TRACKING
/ self trak-ing /
verb

2.5

Using a smartphone to keep track of bodily functions and activities, such as tracking steps, sleep quality, menstrual cycle, and the length of a meditation.

↗

PHUBBING
/ fuhb-ing /
verb

2.5

The practice of ignoring people in a social situation in order to pay attention to one's smartphone.

↗

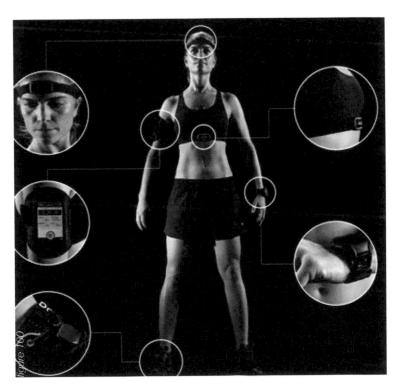
figure 99

figure 100

88

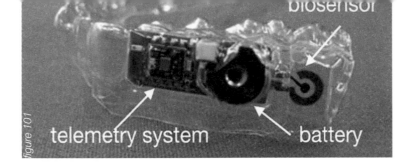

biosensor

telemetry system ~ battery

figure 101

2.6 Am I a smart-phone tourist?

figure 102

↑ *3D Rendering of* **"Trevi Fountain"** *from Thousands of Tourist Photos byNeRF-W technology
/ 2020 /* A team of researchers at Google have come up
with a technique that can combine thousands of tourist
photos into detailed 3D renderings that take you inside
a scene… even if the original photos used vary wildly in
terms of lighting or include other problematic elements
like people or cars.

figure 106

figure 105

figure 107

figure 108

92

SENSE OF SELF

2.7 Should I improve my memory or upgrade my storage? ↗

figure 110

93

↑ *Photo* **"Four months of conversation"**
    by Gray Crawford / 2021 / Patches of long
messages, or rapidfire link sharing thumbnails like the
idiosyncratic landmarks that help orient and navigate.

figure 1.14

figure 1.15

A camera roll analysis.

200 Photos in May

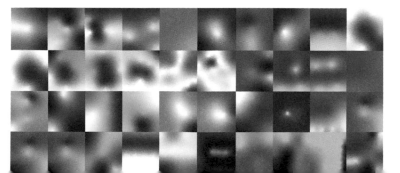

SMARTPHONE AMNESIA

/ smahrt-fohn am-nee- zhuh /

noun

2.7

The tendency to forget information that is or can be stored on the
smartphone, such as friends' phone
numbers and family birthdays.

↗

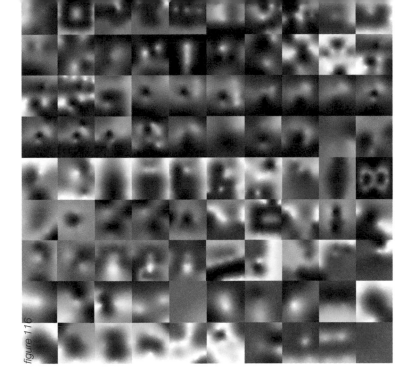
figure 116

2.8 How does my phone see me?

figure 117

figure 118

figure 119

figure 120

figure 121

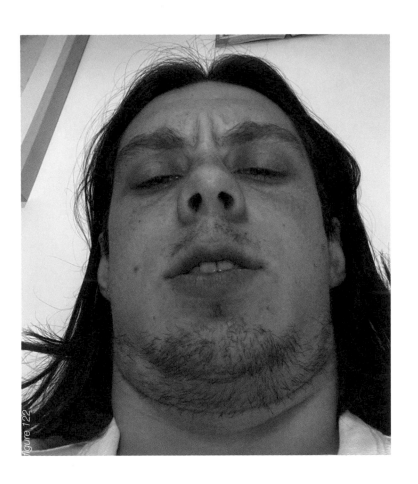

figure 122

figure 123

2.9 Felt cute might delete later? ↗

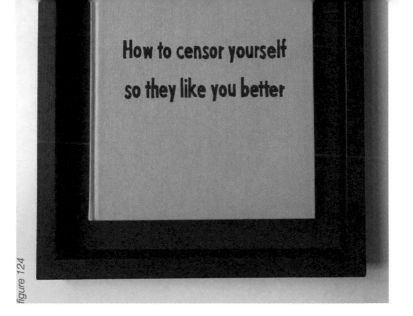

How to censor yourself
so they like you better

figure 124

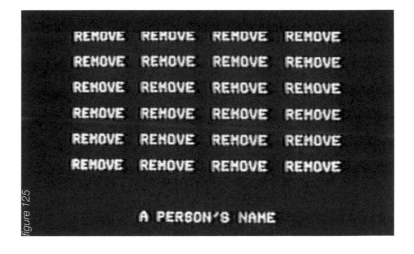

REMOVE REMOVE REMOVE REMOVE
REMOVE REMOVE REMOVE REMOVE
REMOVE REMOVE REMOVE REMOVE
REMOVE REMOVE REMOVE REMOVE
REMOVE REMOVE REMOVE REMOVE
REMOVE REMOVE REMOVE REMOVE

A PERSON'S NAME

figure 125

figure 126

figure 127

This story is no longer available

figure 128

Today

⊘ *You deleted this message.*
18:04

⊘ *You deleted this message.*
18:04

⊘ *You deleted this message.*
18:04

FINSTA

/ fin-sta /

noun

2.9

Someone's alternate profile on social media, which is more personal and candid and can only be followed by their closest friends.

↗

BREADCRUMBING
/ bred-kruhm-ing /
verb

2.9

The practice of leading someone on by sporadically leaving them with a text message, phone call, or social media interaction, often without any follow-through.

↗

MY LOVE,

The day Prometheus breathed life into the new me, was the day you arrived in a little box. A shiny, futuristic black box, Pandora's box, despite my doubts I couldn't help but open it to finally meet you. Doubts, because I was happy with who I was, with who I saw looking at me through the eyes of others I presented myself to in everyday life. But I was seduced by the worlds that were promised to me if I let you into my life, who I would be with you in my pocket.

As soon as the lid came off and I swiped my fingers over your radiant surface for the first time, the world and I were bursting at the seams. What a creation we were together, to what sizes we grew! My brain an encyclopedia, my body an unerring compass, my eyes and ears reaching infinitely with you as an extension of myself. Through you, I, the cyborg, could enter bewildering virtual spaces in which I was presently absent, meanwhile absently present in the material world of boring train rides, waiting lines, and mindless chit chats with others. I felt invincible, transformed into a citizen of the world because of you, an intellectual of unimaginable proportions for the vast sea of knowledge you allowed me to surf on, a public speaker and influencer of significance because my words and visual snippets of my days could be launched into the world with the flick of a finger, likes enticing and confirming me. How intoxicating! How wonderfully, pleasantly intoxicating!

But I can't help but sometimes lie awake at night, my internal clock slowing down with your seductive blue light illuminating my face with 2,457,600 (1920x1080) LED suns. In those moments, as my eyes are captivated by your glow, I can't help thinking about the time before you arrived, and how I sometimes miss my low definition self. You are always there, sometimes it feels like we are in fact one – finally reunited with my other Plato's half, fused into not a circle but a perfect black rectangle. Through your eyes I see the world and myself in Ultra-HD, my pixel density has never been so high.

But you are sometimes vicious, my dear – a viper, a temptress, when then again with sweet codes you reflect my most beautiful self, and I cannot help but love me through your gaze, then again with suffocating algorithms you fragment my self and blow it up to grotesque self-distortions, hurling me into an endless me-loop, that eventually disgusts and alienates me. In those moments you are a distorting mirror, a frightening black box, a black hole that swallows my attention in ways I can't see through. I see my old self disappearing in the vague, dark reflection of myself, with double chin and dull eyes, which I sometimes catch in your black glass when your suns stop dazzling me for a split second. And I can't help but wonder if my 'self' in times of its digital recombination, in which the 'I' is a fragmented multitude of pixels that never fully touch at their sides, a simulacrum, maybe has lost some of its aura.

But in the morning all is forgotten, my love, all is well. As soon as we merge back into one, as soon as I, panicked, reach for my pocket on the train, only to discover with a glow of relief that you were there after all, I can't imagine an "I" without you. Artificial by nature my self resides within your screen, I would be lost without you.

HABITS ☺

The user is habituated to their smartphone. Their everyday life is arranged by the functionalities of their essential device. The user has a personal assistant, an extension of their body, and with that the user moves through their day more swiftly. By easing life's struggles, the smartphone has made the user both lazy and quick, numb and creative, and is shifting and shaping their daily habits by its almost invisible yet unmissable presence.

3

3.1 How religiously do you use your phone?

figure 129

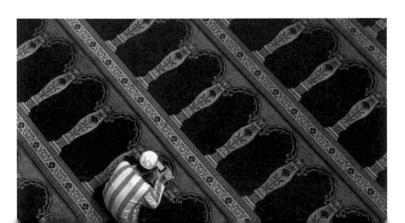

↑ *Photo of Pope Francis by unknown author / January 16,* 2016 */* Pope Francis blesses the child's image through his mobile phone, during the audience in Sala Nervi at the Christian Workers Movement

3.2 Do I have a text neck? ↗

figure 135

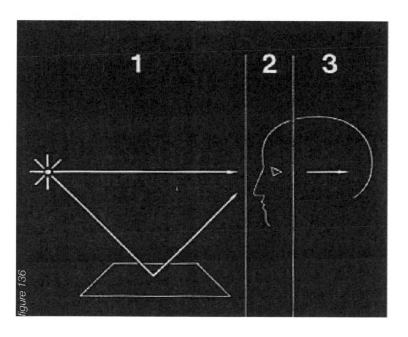

figure 136

1   2   3

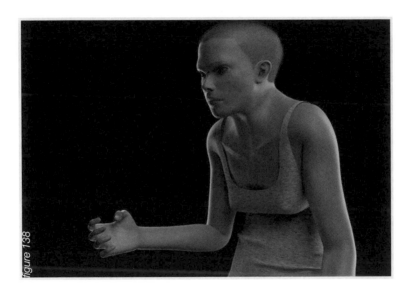

figure 137

figure 138

3D model **"Mindy"** by *TollFreeForwarding.com* / 2019 / Mindy is a 3D model of a human from the year 2100 based on scientific predictions and has developed a hunched back, a shrunken brain, and a second set of eyelids to cope with the sustained use of technology devices.

114

figure 139

figure 140

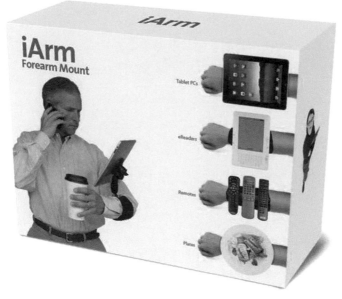

TEXT NECK
/ tekst nek /
noun

3.2

The posture formed by leaning forward for prolonged periods due to smartphone-use, resulting in stress, neck and shoulder pain, and headaches.

↗

SMOMBIE
/ smom-bee /
noun

3.2

A pedestrian using a smart-phone who is oblivious to the world around them, a smartphone zombie.

↗

figure 141

3.3 Can I bring my phone to the spa? ↗

figure 142

figure 143

figure 145

figure 146

120

CHECKING HABIT
/ chek-ing hab-it /
noun

3.3

The automated behavior of quickly opening the smartphone to check for new notifications on the standby screen or content in a specific application.

↗

3.4 Does texting count as a work-out? ↗

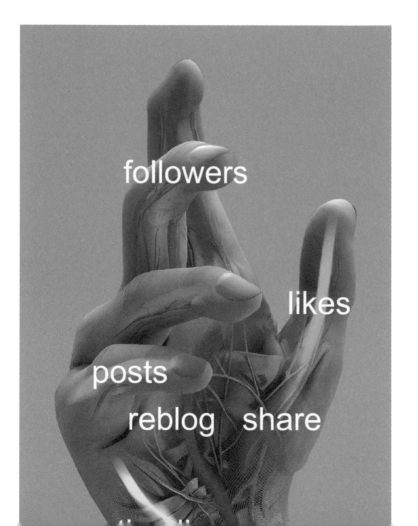

followers

likes

posts

reblog   share

timeline

figure 147

Me when I use my phone daily

Me before I owned a phone

figure 148

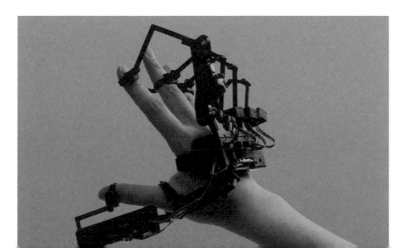

what it feels like texting from a desktop

figure 150

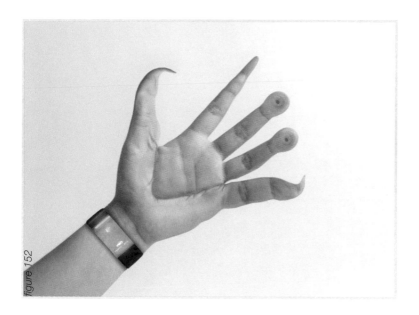

Illustration **"What our hands might look like if they evolved for cellphone use"** *by Broad-bandchoices* / 2017 / A pointy index finger would help with navigation, the mobile phone comparison team that came up with the images determined. Gel pads on the tips of some of your fingers would let you clutch your phone more securely.

TEXT CLAW
/ tekst klaw /
noun

3.4

A non-medical term describing the cramping of all fingers, due to excessive gaming, scrolling and texting on smartphones.

figure 153

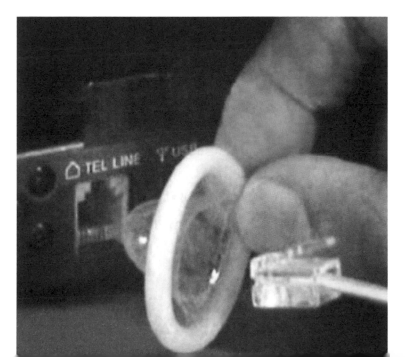

3.5 What is safe-sexting? ↗

figure 15

Decode your teen's TXT lingo!

More than 85% of teenagers use cell phones every day. Use this guide to
figure out their secret "text code" and keep them out of trouble.

figure 155

DLOD: Doing Lots Of Drugs
SBBQ: Sex Barbecue
OMGB: Old Man Gangbang
PSMD: Parents Suck Mad D.*
NMH: Need More Heroin
PMC: Prolapsing My Colon
LKAB: Let's Kill A Bum
MHIO: My Hole Is Open

* Dick

figure 156

Trust This Person?

Your feelings and energy will be accessible to this person when connected.

figure 157

Trust	Don't Trust

SEXTING
/ seks-ting /
verb

3.5

A non-medical term describing the cramping of all fingers, due to excessive gaming, scrolling and texting on smartphones.

figure 158

3.6 **Do I need a partner if I have a phone?**

figure 159

figure 161

figure 162

figure 16

132

figure 163

3.7 **Can my pet take my selfies?**

figure 164

figure 165

figure 166

134

Figure 16.?

3.8 Does my phone make me lazy?

7:25AM
Alarm

Image **"Good morning"** by Pablo Rochat
/ 2019 /

figure 168

figure 169

Quick Reactions

figure 170

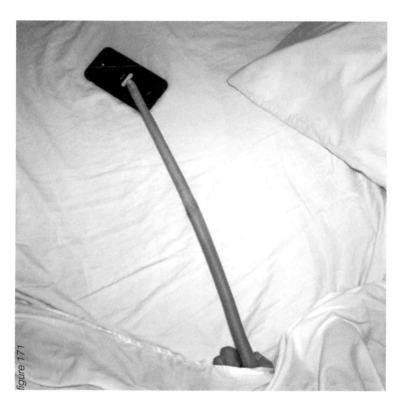

figure 171

figure 172

 Pray For (55) **Pray Against (136)**

figure 173

figure 174

3.9 How much is too much screen time? ↗

figure 175

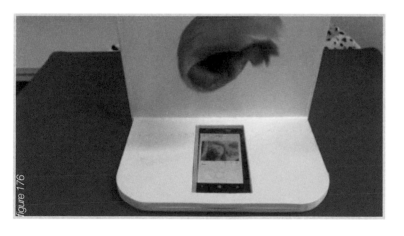

figure 176

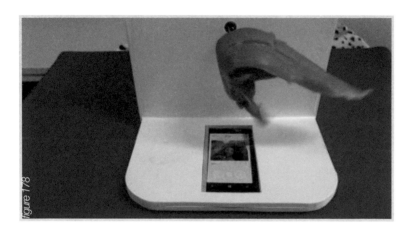

figure 177

figure 178

↑ *Shots from* **"Tender - It's how people meat"** *by Marcello Gómez Maureira /* 2015 */ Tender is* the easy way to connect with new and interesting meat around you. Switch on and if someone likes you back, it's a match!

figure 179

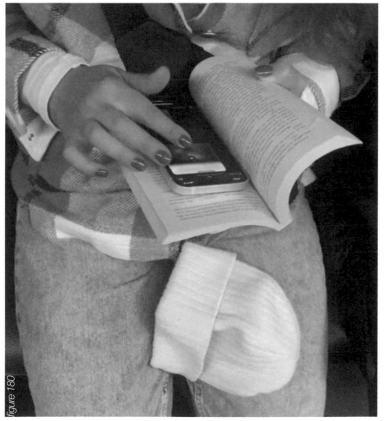

figure 180

SCREENTIME

/ skreen-tahym /

noun

3.9

The amount of time a smart-phone-user spends looking at or interacting with content on their smartphone screen.

↗

SKIM READING
/ skim ree-ding /
verb

3.9

The practice of reading a text by only skimming through it on a smartphone in order to quickly find what we need.

I look through people's phones when they leave them unattended

I've been looking through people's phones for years. Ex-significant others, friends, even a random person at one point. I first would just go into my SOs phone and look through texts, looking to see if there was anything suspicious or if they were cheating on me. One time I did find something, but never confronted them about it. I would read through texts with their friends, and one time I found a nude picture of the friend. After that, I began looking through phones for nude pictures, and then reading through texts. At first it was just SOs, then it turned into friends' phones when they would leave their phone unattended or sleeping. Sometimes I would have to guess the password. It always felt wrong but the feeling of getting into another person's phone was so exhilarating, and when I found what I was looking for it all paid off. I've been doing this for years and no one ever caught me. I covered my tracks perfectly every time. I saw many pictures I was never meant to see. I read many conversations I was never supposed to read. I knew things about my peers I was never supposed to know.

One night of drinking with my friends, I noticed a phone was just lying around. I decided to take this phone and hide in the bathroom to see if I could get in. I succeeded. I then quickly left the gathering and "went to sleep". I waited till everyone was asleep, and then began looking through the phone. I had found what I was looking for. My friends had spent a couple hours after I "went to sleep" looking for the phone, but eventually gave up saying they would look when they were sober in the morning. After I went through the phone, I placed it in a very obvious spot. In the morning, they had found it, obviously confused as to why they couldn't find it the previous night. As the day went on, my friends continued to wonder what had happened.

144

Sometime that evening, my friend confronted me. They had said someone had been on their phone, and they saw activity in the early hours of the day. They saw the apps I went through, which was every app, and asked what I was doing. I confessed. Idk why I did this but as soon as I saw the phone unattended I just could only think about how I could sneak away with it.

As a result, my friends do no longer speak to me. I'm seeking therapy and have moved out of the residence I was living in. I felt like I could do anything, that I was craft and sneaky enough that I could dupe my friends. I feel like shit but I have been feeling like a shitty person for years. I just feel the most remorse for breaking the trust and respect of my friends.

posted by u/jjhumperdink
on Reddit

During long layovers I do "airdrop drive-bys" to random iPhones

I've found the best way to pass time while on long layovers. I'll walk around crowded terminals looking for iPhones with Bluetooth turned on, and I'll send them random weird pictures. Nothing pornographic or extremely repulsive... just random. I then wait for phones to accept the photos and try to figure out who accepted them by watching the reactions on people's faces. I don't feel extremely bad about it but I did witness an old woman react to the photo I sent. I took a picture while traveling and started sending it to random phones while waiting for a delayed flight. The gate area wasn't extremely packed so I was easily able to watch people's faces. One phone accepted the photo so I started my search. I noticed an older woman, maybe 70 or so, look at her screen then all around the gate. Then back to the screen. Then she nudged her travel partner and showed them. They both looked perplexed and started looking around. I put the phone down and took off walking.

I regularly pretend I am talking to someone on the phone

I regularly pick up my phone and pretend to talk to someone about something important just to avoid unpleasant situations. Sometimes I talk for minutes and really get into it. I found out that it actually helps me developing ideas as I sometimes discuss what's on my mind with my imaginary caller. And pretending to discuss a specific topic helps me to come up with new arguments that'll did not think of before. Right now I am at this huge event hosted by my company and I am the only company sponsored student here. So in order to look busy, I just had a three-minute phone call with my boss about some really important project. Well that led to an awesome conversation with a colleague about a similar project... I guess it's not that bad after all! 😶

RESOURCES

The user carries a device that sources its power from the natural world. During the first stages of its development, during the time it is used, and the time it will never be used again, the smartphone has an influence on the world as the user knows it, by leaving its traces as it lends from everything it comes across. Wherever it goes, the smartphone claims supplies of elements and energy, with the user as one of its resources.

4.1   Who touched my phone before me?

figure 181

Figure 183

figure 18

figure 185

↑ *Image from series* **"Friends of the Earth"** *by Ulet Ifansasti* / 2013 / Febri Andika, a young tin miner, searches for tin ore at a mine in Belo Laut village.

figure 187

4.2 How many phones do we need?

figure 189

Image **"Pokémon GO"** *by u/jkevintu /* 2019 /
The Pokémon GO grandpa now has 45 phones
on his bike.

↑ *Performance and installation* **"Google Maps Hacks"** *by Simon Weckert* / Berlin, 2020 / 99 secondhand smartphones were transported in a hand-cart to generate virtual traffic jams in Google Maps.

figure 194

figure 195

4.3 What energy do phones use/ run on?

figure 196

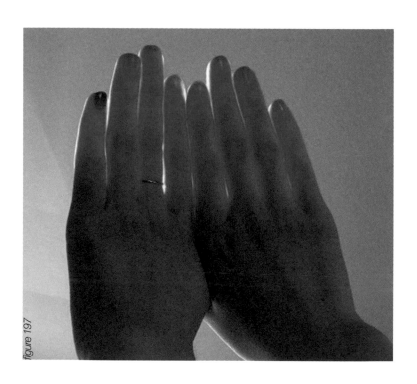
figure 197

158

figure 198

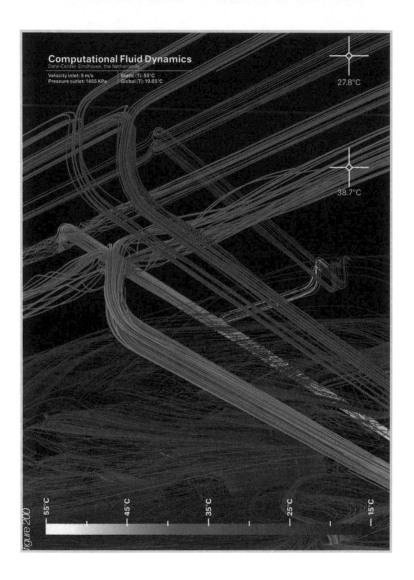

Computational Fluid Dynamics
Data-Center, Eindhoven, the Netherlands

Velocity inlet: 5 m/s | Static (T): 55°C
Pressure outlet: 1455 KPa | Global (T): 19.85°C

27.8°C

38.7°C

55°C — 45°C — 35°C — 25°C — 15°C

Project **"Bathing in the Cloud - Computational Fluid Dynamics"** *by Lucas de Ruiter* / 2020 /

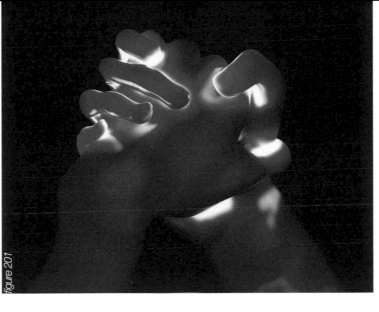

figure 201

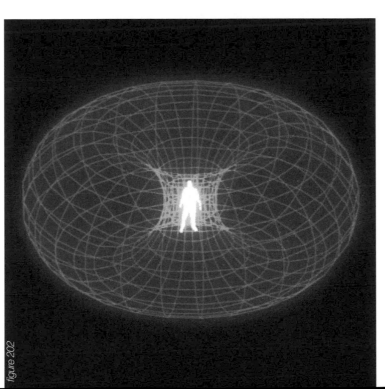

figure 202

4.4 Do I have WiFi here? ↗

figure 204

figure 205

figure 206

figure 207

164

ALWAYS-ON
/ awl-weyz on /
noun

4.4

The experience of being, or needing to be, continually available due to the ubiquitous and intrusive connectivity of the smartphone.

SMARTPHONE STRAIN
/ smahrt-fohn streyn /
noun

4.4

The experience of dry eyes,
blurred vision, and headaches due to
excessive time looking at a smartphone
screen.

↗

figure 208

4.5 How do I up-grade my phone?

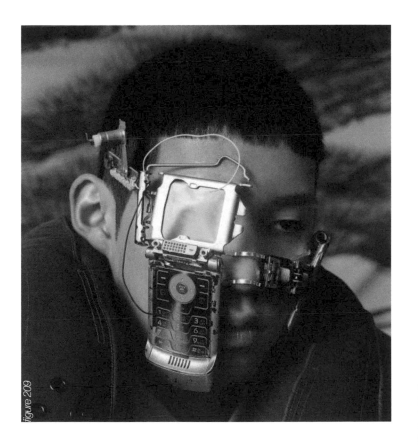

figure 209

figure 210

figure 211

168

figure 212

↑ *Candleholder* **"Post-tech flame"** *by Teresa Fernande Zpello* / Electronic waste material 43,5 x 10 x h42,5 cm, 2020 /

figure 213

figure 214

figure 215

170

4.6 **Am I data?** ↗

figure 217

figure 218

☑ **I have read and accept the** privacy policy *

Facebook's approach to data collection

YOU

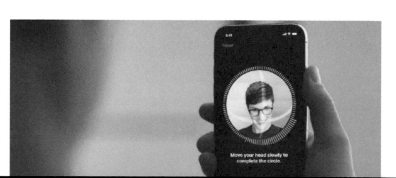

FACE ID
/ feys-ahy-dee /
noun

4.6

A facial recognition and authentication technology that allows users to unlock their smartphone or unlock more specific functionalities of the smartphone by using their face.

↗

4.7 Will the smartphone ever go out of fash-ion? ↗

figure 222

figure 223

figure 224

figure 225

Personal Communicator **"Simon"** by IBM
/ 1992 /

figure 228

figure 229

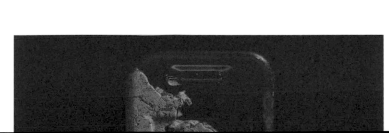

figure 22.

SWIPE

/ swahyp /

verb

4.7

To move (one's finger) across a touchscreen in order to activate a function on the smartphone.

↗

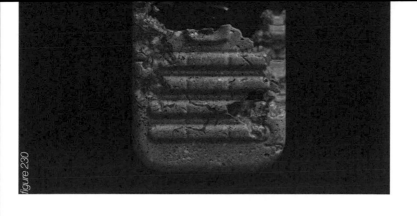

figure 230

4.8   Is my phone safer than a pig-gy bank?

figure 231

figure 232

New payment options for buying IPHONE 11

figure 233

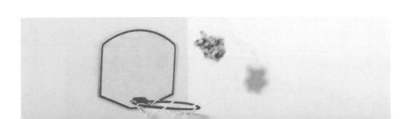

figure 234

figure 23

figure 236

4.9 What will we leave behind?

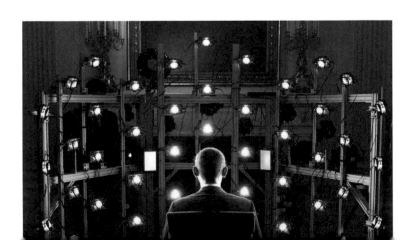

figure 237

figure 238

figure 239

Delete 553 photos from 56 bursts, and 30,743 other items?

These items will be deleted from iCloud Photos on all your devices.

Delete 31,296 Items

Cancel

figure 243

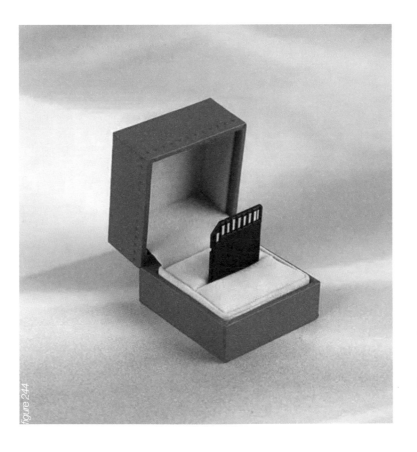

figure 244

Essay by
Chloë Arkenbout

Confessions of a Political Meme Maker

White supremacists got a permit for a protest to spread their oppressive ideology, so a group of leftists - antifa activists, anti-racists organizations, a few local political parties - decided to counter the protest with their own today. Naturally I joined. Apart from the verbal confrontations with scumbags and the disproportionate amount of police violence we encounter in peaceful protests like these, being with this community usually gives me a sense of belonging. I mean, seeing your friends and meeting like-minded people who care about the same things as you do is pretty hopeful. Not today though. You see, ever since I've started making political memes things have changed.

I saw at least 9 people today who I talk to online regularly - some I even consider friends. I don't think I have ever felt so alone though, because they don't know who I am. I get multiple death threats by right-wing extremists in my DM every week, so my anonymous profile literally ensures my safety. If they figure out who I am or where I live then… Some of my close friends don't even know about my memes, because I can't risk it. I know they would be proud of me, but they could never tell me. Talking to other meme makers online, even when I don't even know what they look like, helps a little. But still, when I meet someone new and they ask me 'hey, what do you do as an activist?', I can't tell them the whole truth.

The truth is that I am a genius and that my memes go viral multiple times a week. Prominent activists and politicians share my work all the time. That countless followers told me that they went to their first protest because of me, that they've joined unions, signed petitions, changed their voting behavior or finally got the nerve to confront family members and friends who make hurtful jokes. That I use memes to show the other side of the story when mainstream media publish problematic articles and journalists often ask me for feedback. That my memes make marginalized people feel less alone. That they make me feel less alone.

However, I am also tired all. the. time. I spend hours deleting racist, queerphobic, sexist, and ableist comments, because I want my account to be as safe as possible. Today alone I got 28 DM's from strangers who think my tone is too aggressive as well. Having to explain my human rights to all of them while staying polite, day in and day out, literally drains me. On top of that I also found out yesterday that the General Intelligence and Security Service of my government has listed me as a threat and that they have been watching me. I haven't done anything wrong except for questioning power... I haven't slept all night. I even feel weird using my phone right now.

Perhaps I shouldn't even be spending this much time online anyway. I'm not sure if it's worth it as I'm being shadowbanned again. My story reach has been lower and I don't know what caused it. I don't think I have posted anything too radical lately. I might be close to losing my account permanently. What if I have to start all over again? Should I even be on this capitalist platform that tries to censor critical thinking? Should I just focus on direct action? Take it to the streets? Do memes even change anything? Does anything I do matter? I don't know. We're doomed anyway. I'm off to sleep.

This diary entry is entirely fictional but it is based on the real experiences of various leftist meme creators that I have spoken to for previous research purposes, some of whom I have gotten to know well. A special thanks to them, they know who they are.

EXISTENTIAL CRISIS ☺

The user has reached a point
of pondering on the meaning
of life with a smartphone. In an
attempt to make sense of this
existential crisis, the user tries
to escape real life by switching
to the digital world, only to find
a new existence, in a world
even more abstract. This crisis
state leaves the user feeling
alienated from the one thing
they thought to be sure of:
their smartphone.

5

5.1 Are we getting closer or drifting apart? ↗

figure 245

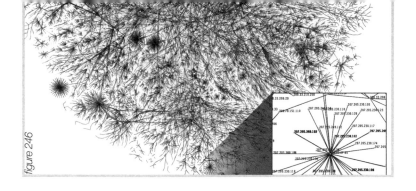

figure 246

↑ *Project* **"Opte"** *by Barrett Lyon / 2005 / visualization of routing paths through a portion of the Internet*

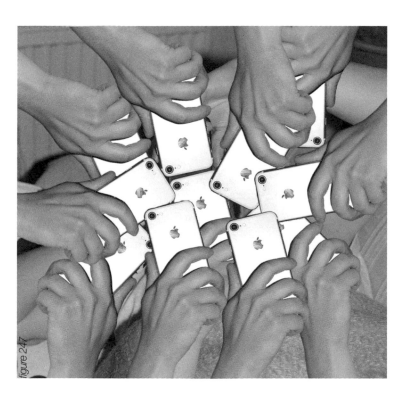

figure 247

figure 248

Chat with a Live Person

figure 249

figure 250

TELEPHOBIA
/ te-le-foh-bee-uh /
noun

5.1

The avoidance and reluctance of taking and making phone calls due to fear and anxiety.

↗

TECHNOFERENCE

/ tek-noh-feer-uhns /

noun

5.1

Everyday interruptions in inter-
personal interactions or time spent
together due to mobile technology
devices.

↗

5.2 Why do anime characters use flip phones instead of smartphones?

figure 251

figure 252

figure 253

196

Figure 254
Figure 255

5.3 What is the size of the Internet?

so much internet
so little time

so litt|e time

figure 256

HAHAHAHAHAHAHAHAHAHAHAHAHAHAHAHAHA

figure 257

198

figure 258

figure 259

The only way out is in.

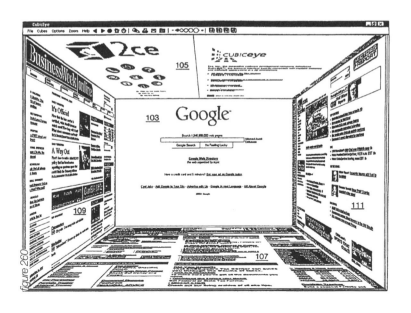

figure 260

SELF-ACTUALIZATION
Pursue Inner Talent
Creativity Fulfillment

SELF-ESTEEM
Achievement Mastery
Recognition Respect

BELONGING - LOVE
Friends Family Spouse Lover

SAFETY
Security Stability Freedom from Fear

PHYSIOLOGICAL
Food Water Shelter Warmth

WiFi

BATTERY

figure 261

Image **"Updated Maslow's hierarchy of needs"** *by Vala Afshar / 2014 /*

ALL THESE
OPEN
WINDOWS,
BUT NO
FRESH AIR.

figure 262

5.4 **Do my on-line actions have real-life conse-quences?** ↗

figure 264

figure 265

↑ *Installation* **"Skittles"** *by Josh Kline* / Commercial refrigerator, light box and blended liquids in bottles, 2014 / With titles like "Big Data" the indigestible "drinks" in this glowing cooler make plain the ways in which our bodies have been engineered, chemically altered, and transformed by technologies of consumption.

figure 266

figure 267

figure 268

204

DEEP LIKE
/ deep - lahyk /
noun

EXISTENTIAL CRISIS

5.4

The like given on an old photo when lurking on someone's social networking profile, accidentally or on purpose to get the person's attention.

205

↗

GHOSTING

/ goh-sting /
verb

5.4

The practice of cutting off all communication with a person without warning or prior notice, mostly done by ignoring phone calls, text messages and removing the person on social media.

↗

5,5 What lies beyond my phone's screen?

figure 269

figure 2

figure 2/1

Augmented Reality **"The Last Statement T-shirt"** *by Virtue* / 2019 / The wearer can choose from a range of graphics created especially for The Last Statement T-shirt and accessible through the Instagram or Facebook apps, where it works on the same principle as face filters.

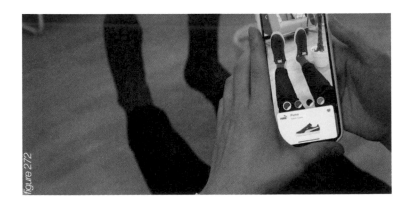

figure 2/2

figure 273

Augmented Reality **"Museum From Home"** *by Cuseum* / 2020 / Users will be able to virtually place paintings and other objects onto their walls and revel in artworks that are typically only available to view inside a museum setting.

figure 274

5.6 Can I find 'spiritual journey' on Google Maps? ↗

figure 275

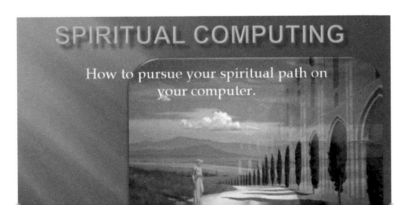

SPIRITUAL COMPUTING

How to pursue your spiritual path on your computer.

TECHNOSELF
/ tek-no-self /
noun

5.6

The self that views reality through technology, altering our perception of the activity of ourselves and others to fit the smartphone, for example deciding which route to walk home based on the amount of steps it will log onto our phone, instead of based on the nice views.

↗

figure 277

5.7 Do birds tweet?

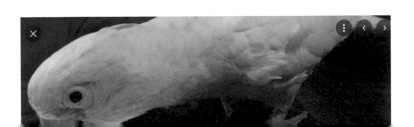

figure 278

I'm very concerned that our society is much more interested in information than wonder.

figure 279

figure 280

5.8 Are there more emojis than emotions?

figure 281

figure 283

	Emoticon			Emoji		
	Low	Moderate	High	Low	Moderate	High
Aesthetical Appeal	L-) Emot46	(^.^) Emot17e	:) Emot18a	 EmjAp73	EmjAn03	EmjAp71
Familiarity	[-(Emot24	:-* Emot13b	;) Emot08a	EmjAn52	EmjAp50	EmjFb76
Visual Complexity	:-) Emot18c	(^_~) Emot08d	~X(Emot81	EmjAp40	EmjAn18	EmjAn89
Clarity	O Emot19a	:-/ Emot45c	:)) Emot01c	EmjAp24	EmjAn28	EmjAp05
Valence	:(Emot40a	d-_-b Emot76b	<3 Emot71	EmjAn68	EmjFb29	EmjAp04
Arousal	-_-zzZ Emot34b	:">\ Emot09	:'(Emot56a	EmjAp34	EmjAn08	EmjAp67
Meaningfulness	=; Emot75	:b Emot37c	:D Emot01a	EmjAn24	EmjAn23	EmjAp12

Fig. 4 Sample emoticons and emoji for each level across dimensions (LEED stimulus codes are included). For valence: low = negative, moderate = neutral, high = positive

figure 284

VOCABULARY £

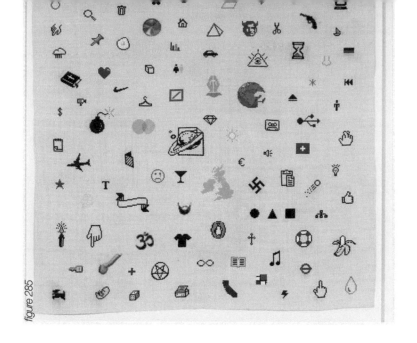

figure 285

Art piece **"Vocabulary"** *by Simon Evans* / Hand woven paper 187.4 X 143.5 cm, 2011 /

figure 286

figure 287

5.9 Will my phone ever fit inside my pocket? ↗

figure 288

figure 289

figure 29[
figure 291

5.10 Is my phone an altar? ↗

figure 292

figure 293

figure 295

figure 296

BRICK PHONE

/ brik fohn /
noun

5.9

Early cell phones invented by
Martin Cooper in the 90's that resem-
bled bricks due to their size, weight
and rectangular cuboid shape.

↗

PHANTOM VIBRATION
/ fan-tuhm vahy-brey-shuhn /
noun

5.10

The perception that one's mobile phone is vibrating or ringing when it is not.

↗

5.11 Is there life after the smart-phone?

figure 297

Michael A.
Stoos

Jan. 31,
1970

Mar. 14,
2010

at&t

THERESA SIFAGA

↑ *Headstone in shape of iPhone for Theresa Matautia* / New Zealand, 2022 / "When our sister died, we made her phone her headstone because she was always on it," her brother explains.

figure 301

THANK YOU FOR ENGAGING WITH MY CONTENT

figure 302

ABOUT THE AUTHORS

Chloë Arkenbout explores the tactics used by marginalized communities to shift oppressive discourses in the digital world. At the Institute of Network Cultures, a research group at the Amsterdam University of Applied Sciences, she focuses on viral image culture and co-edited two readers on critical meme research. Her research and teaching topics range from speculative design to call out culture - but political memes remain her expertise. Which is why, for SWIPE, she made an imaginative leap into the mind of a political meme-maker.

Ruben Baart is the editor-in-chief at Next Nature. He operates at the intersection of design, science and technology. Among other projects, Ruben edited Next Nature Magazine, 50 Products from the Future and Future Food; art, science and technology.

Mieke Gerritzen is a designer, producer, and administrator. Until 2017 she was the Director of Museum of the Image, MOTI in Breda. She then founded the Image Society. She initiates and organizes debates, exhibitions, and events with designers, artists, and authors about image culture, design and new media. There are more than 10 books to her name. Since 2022 Gerritzen works as creative lead for Next Nature. miekegerritzen.com

Ieva Jakusa is an independent designer specializing in creative direction. Her interest lies in technology and human interaction. Throughout her multi-disciplinary approach, she focuses on creative strategy and how to capture and re-frame what is already there. Ieva is an alumnus of Design Academy Eindhoven and has participated in such events as Dutch Design Week, Salon de Mobile, and several group exhibitions.

Beau Magdelijns is an editor and writer, interested in the way non-digital phenomena become increasingly digitized, and the way culture both influences and is influenced by this process. She graduated cum laude from New Media & Digital Culture at Utrecht University with her thesis on the neoliberal nature of digital therapy apps. During her studies, Beau worked as an intern for Next Nature, for which she wrote and co-edited SWIPE.

Elize de Mul explores the influence of using contemporary technologies on human identity and privacy, by combining her expert knowledge on both philosophy and new media studies. Her previous work is a philosophical reflection on humans' relationship to a widely used but seemingly insignificant thing: the plastic bag. In doing the latter, Elize offers the object a face, a personality, like she does in her love letter to the smartphone for SWIPE.

Henk Oosterling approaches the world from the understanding that thinking and philosophizing are practices that are continually intertwined with and inseparable from the environment. As an ecosopher - a portmanteau of ecology and philosopher - he argues that what is central to our thoughts and practices should not be our ego, but our eco. Henk follows this line of thought for SWIPE as he argues that the changing human ecology in the current Anthropocene, due to the smartphone's ubiquity in our environment, is in need of new literacies to refocus on the use of social media.

CREDITS

figure 1 Concepttalk. Simpler Times. Nokia 3310. Instagram, 2021. https://www.instagram.com/p/CWrMi-YnsM8D/

figure 2 Timothy Prickett Morgan. BIG BLUE AIMS FOR THE SKY WITH POWER9: Power9. NextPlatform, 2016. https://www.nextplatform.com/2016/08/24/big-blue-aims-sky-power9/

figure 3 2stepsback. Screenshot from Workrave - Repetitive Strain Injury prevention software. DonationCoder, 2007. https://www.donationcoder.com/forum/index.php?topic=8192.0

figure 4 Kare Susan. Sketch and code for Apple graphic user icon. Apple Inc., Firm,1983. https://www.sfmoma.org/artwork/2017.479/

figure 5 Bugus. Don't Hit My Phone (Prod. Paul Maxwell). Song Cover Picture. YouTube, 2017. https://www.youtube.com/watch?v=PmO8UQ-hsYc

figure 6 Satccaptures. Screenshot from Sex and the City. Tumblr, 2012. satccaptures.tumblr.com (not existing anymore) otherwise, the oldes resource is here https://bonjour.ba/legendarne-scene-carrie-bradshaw

figure 7 LoopyCases, Storage Compartment Phone Case. FindGoodLive, 2014. https://www.findgoodlive.com/?product_id=44143373_27

figure 8 Tonycapp. Keep This in Your Back Pocket, It May Come in Handy. Reddit, R/amcstock, 2021. https://preview.redd.it/mt7mmt4h0tv61.jpg?auto=webp&s=7bb1314b30b39ba1449a5fc056666647a5b9030

figure 9 Cnossen Maggie. Smart Phone. Mixed media scanography on iPhone X. MaggieCnossen, 2019. https://maggiecnossen.com/Smart-Phone

figure 10 Zvedeng. ZVE Multifunctional Cigarette Lighter Cover for iPhone 6 iPhone 6s with Built-in Cigarette Lighter Bottle Opener Heavy Duty Shockproof Case. Amazon, 2015. https://www.amazon.co.uk/ZVE-Multifunctional-Cigarette-Lighter-Shockproof/dp/B00YIDA3AW

figure 11 Gharabli Ahmad. A Palestinian woman takes a picture of a member of the Israeli security forces as she takes her picture in a street in Jerusalem. December 16, 2017. Getty images. https://www.gettyimages.com/detail/news-photo/s-palestinian-photojournalist-ahmad-gharablis-striking-news-photo/1139207914?adppopup=true

figure 12 Frazier Darnella. Derek Chauvin kneeling on George Floyd's neck in Minneapolis. May 25, 2020. Originaly posted on Facebook May 26, 2020, later removed. https://www.nbcnews.com/news/us-news/minneapolis-police-officer-center-george-floyd-s-death-had-history-n1215691

figure 13 kbaig. Little Handala. Blogspot, 2011. http://state-terrorist.blogspot.com/2011/08/children-of-palestine-in-pictures.html

figure 14 UkraineWorld. Ukrainian woman confronts Russian soldiers in Henychesk, Kherson region. Twitter, 2022. https://twitter.com/futureboy/status/1496999905839050757

figure 15 Elvert Barnes. Protest Photography. Baltimore Women's March Gathering Rally at War Memorial Plaza at 101 North Gay Street in Baltimore, Maryland, January 20, 2018. https://commons.wikimedia.org/w/index.php?curid=65897789

figure 16 C.M. Pride Protest. Twitter, 2022. https://pbs.twimg.com/media/FWsDY3sXwAlpxk1?format=jpg&name=large

figure 17 papas_imaculate. Protest Photography in Sri Lanka. Twitter, July 9, 2022. https://pbs.twimg.com/media/FXP_KNUWIAIU6jr?format=jpg&name=medium

figure 18 CathLAndrews. Protest Photography in US. Twitter, July 2, 2022. https://twitter.com/CathLAndrews/status/1543136717754204161?s=20&t=9bU12vbx-gE9OtdNlru7Wlg

figure 19 Morgan Sutherland. Untitled. Are.na, 2016. https://d2w9rnfcy7mm78.cloudfront.net/274996/original_96dd16eaee2526926ff72f7ab-510f9ab?1410048101?bc=1

figure 20 Chris Jackson. The Prince of Wales and The Duchess of Cornwall Tour Oman - Day 1. Getty Images, 2016. https://www.gettyimages.nl/detail/nieuwsfoto%27s/dancer-tucks-his-apple-iphone-next-to-his-traditional-nieuws-fotos/621189392?adppopup=true

figure 21 Author unknown. Chinese Phone Reviews. Gifsf, 2021. https://gifsf.com/humor_new1/4619961

figure 22 In1 Multi-Tool Utility Case. Instagram, 2016. https://www.instagram.com/p/BANO2ULvO-P/?taken-by=in1case

figure 23 Arc M Sch. Weapon X stick, dental floss, computer chip. Are.na, 2017. https://d2w9rnfcy7mm78.cloudfront.net/941402/original_0e11b6fc077a0da-fa67a229b2ac51bb1.jpg?1490389939?bc=1

figure 24 Barry Bland. Pigeon Post. Daily Mail, 2009. https://www.dailymail.co.uk/news/article-1224522/Pigeon-post-Meet-birds-backpack-deliver-parcels-time.html

figure 25 James Bayard. Installation "txt me when u get here". Are.na, 2010. https://www.are.na/block/1265629

figure 26 Piximus. Odd Situations. April, 2022. https://piximus.net/others/odd-situations

figure 27 Scott Kelly and Ben Polkinghorne. Mountain - Temporary Installation. New Plymouth, New Zealand. 2016. https://www.scottconradkelly.com/signs-of-the-times

figure 28 Author Unknown. CTRL+Z RUBBER, CTRL+V TAPE, CTRL+X SCISSORS meme. StareCat, 2022. https://starecat.com/ctrlz-rubber-ctrlv-tape-ctrlx-scissors/

figure 29 Andrea Vincze. Shot from a video Woman follows GPS; ends up in Ontario lake. May 2016. https://www.dailymail.co.uk/news/article-3590775/Scuba-driver-Woman-suffers-excruciating-GPS-fail-drives-100-feet-freezing-Ontario-lake.html

figure 30 Uglydesign. AirPods3000. Instagram, 2019. https://www.instagram.com/p/BtbSu1_ILLW/?utm_source=ig_embed&ig_rid=a7e8beae-963e-4dd5-be18-8b1f60bf0b50

figure 31 Kim Laughton. Image. Tumbrl, 2014. https://

kimlaughton.tumblr.com/post/84627318899

figure 32 Tegan Davis. tru3158537.jpg. Arena, 2022. https://www.are.na/block/15477956

figure 33 Sophiyah E. with Detroit Bureau of Sound, and 3k. Poolside Performance: Phonosynthesis. Cranbrook Art Museum, US, June 23, 2022. https://seenthemagazine.com/event/poolside-performance-phonosynthesis/

figure 34 Garry Ing. karrabing-film-kollektive-rory-pilgrim-at-kunstverein-braunschweig-10.jpg. Are.na, 2021. https://d2w9rnfcy7mm78.cloudfront.net/12765706/original_201e1eadc8f831c892d5949b9701a81e.jpg?1628259058?bc=0

figure 35-44 AI image generator. Foldable futuristic smartphone. DALL·E mini, July 12, 2022. https://huggingface.co/spaces/dalle-mini/dalle-mini

figure 45 Akihiro Yoshida. Nendo sliding-phone concept for OPPO. Nendo, 2020. https://www.nendo.jp/en/works/slide-phone/?

figure 46 Akihiro Yoshida. Nendo sliding-phone concept for OPPO. Nendo, 2020. https://www.nendo.jp/en/works/slide-phone/?

figure 47 Special Projects Studio. Envelope. Special Projects Studio, 2020. https://specialprojects.studio/project/envelope/

figure 48 Daniel Rubino. Image of Surface Duo 2. Twitter, July 8, 2022. https://twitter.com/Daniel_Rubino/status/1545447929615368193?s=20&t=j0FAcwat-T2D7k_QXtdBiJQ

figure 49 Image With No Author. Cerium. Images of Elements, 2016. https://images-of-elements.com/cerium.php

figure 50 Image With No Author.Tantalum. Images of Elements, 2016. https://images-of-elements.com/tantalum.php

figure 51 Henri Koskinen. Lithium. Year Unknown. Adobe Images. https://stock.adobe.com/nl/search?k=%22lithium+mineral%22&asset_id=252223739

figure 52 Unknown Author. Cobalt. JD. Year Unknown. https://www.justdial.com/jdmart/Mumbai/Cobalt-Metal-Co/pid-2021032506/022PXX22-XX22-170828200244-Z3I1

figure 53 Unknown Author. Rhodium. Year Unknown. https://s-media-cache-ak0.pinimg.com/564x/98/fd/97/98fd977723ccc65f2d87b644c120eb1.jpg

figure 54 Unknown Author. Cassiterite. Year Unknown. https://www.gemstone7.com/495-cassiterite.html

figure 55 Image With No Author. Tantalum. Images of Elements, 2016. https://images-of-elements.com/tantalum.jpg

figure 56 Din M'rini. Sad cowboy meme. 2017. https://www.reddit.com/r/im14andthisisdeep/comments/92ru9v/masked_by_a_cowboy/

figure 57 Sully Says. You're not deep, You're not an intellectual, You're not an artist, You're not a critic, You're not a poet, You just have internet access. 2010. https://paisleyunderground-blog.tumblr.com/post/659254068/sullysays

figure 58 Screenshot from American Psycho. Procoal, 2018. https://procoal.co.uk/blogs/beauty/the-procoal-american-psycho-patrick-bateman-skincare-routine

figure 59 Author unknown. We're All Sims. Arena, 2018. https://www.are.na/block/1916276

figure 60 Virbela. A snapshot of a the ringbearers delivering the rings through the cloud wedding. Virbela, Courtesy of Traci Gagnon,2021. https://www.insider.com/wedding-ceremony-metaverse-virtual-chapel-avatars-lives-tream-2021-12

figure 61 AlphaSpirit. False and lying husband. https://stock.adobe.com/images/false-and-lying-husband/83565150

figure 62 Image With No Author. User Icon. PNGFind. https://www.pngfind.com/mpng/iiTxhm_user-icon-clip-art-customer-hd-png-download/

figure 63 Abbey Lossing. Title unknown. Medium, 2021. https://medium.com/swlh/want-to-make-a-huge-comeback-then-stop-complaining-766bd2a79757

figure 64 mofu_sand. Cell phone addiction. Instagram, 2021. https://www.instagram.com/p/CK-jPijjnu2b/?igshid=skofeovjynsy

figure 65 Annika Bobb, Neil Turner, and Luis Colindres. Image of dog with smartphone. Dailydot, March 23, 2018. https://www.dailydot.com/unclick/dog-steals-cell-phone/

figure 66 Foshan Nanhai Shengzhuo Toys Factory. Year unknown. Alibaba. https://www.alibaba.com/product-detail/EN71-Europe-standard-new-design-cartoon_60635020325.html

figure 67 Cat playing with smartphone. 2016. https://techweez.com/2016/06/20/slow-down-in-app-downloads/cat-playe-with-smartphone/

figure 68 Caters News Agency. This macaque was in a mischievous mood at the Jigokudani park in Japan and made off with an iPhone. Daily Mail, June 5, 2016. https://www.dailymail.co.uk/news/article-3626284/Now-s-oo-oo-oo-Phone-Cheeky-snow-monkey-grabs-tourist-s-phone-takes-swim.html

figure 69 Image With No Author. If social media collapses i will stand on the street holding up hand painted memes.

figure 70-74 Mvzenxx. Image of dog with smartphone. Twitter. https://twitter.com/mvzenxx/status/687411487174950912?lang=en

figure 75 Unknown Author. Weird Funny Instagram Cats. Cattime, 2019. https://cattime.com/assets/uploads/2019/02/Weird_Funny_Instagram_Cats_Featured.jpg

figure 76 Dima666666789. Wallpaper knife, nutella, phone. Goodfon, January 6, 2016. https://www.goodfon.com/wallpaper/nutella-phone-stol.html

figure 77 Ieva Jakusa. Fridge. Orginal image, 2022.

figure 78 Boo Chapple and Bo Wong. Consumables. Plastic Green: Designing Bio-spatial Futures, 2019. https://www.ediblegeography.com/edible-cellphones/

figure 79 Boo Chapple and Bo Wong. Consumables. Plastic Green: Designing Bio-spatial Futures, 2019. https://www.ediblegeography.com/edible-cellphones/

figure 80 Image With No Author. iPhone with butterknife. Tumblr. Year Unknown.

figure 81 Ada Chen. Text earrings. Instagram, July, 2019. https://www.instagram.com/p/B0MWfQ3FoWd/

figure 82 Kelianne. Crisis of the Real, 04. Kelianne, November, 2016. https://kelianne.com/crisis-of-the-real/

figure 83 Break Rules Not Nails. Techo-Logical. Break Rules Not Nails, June 22, 2014. https://breakrulesnotnails.wordpress.com/2014/06/22/techno-logical/

figure 84 Gab Bois. Photograph Bikinearpods. GabBois, 2021. http://www.gabbois.com/

figure 85 DIS Magazine. iPod Shuffle Hair Clip. Facebook, June 2013. https://m.facebook.com/DISmagazine/photos/a.388569294032/10151495492049033/?_se_imp=295o3OTqRzGKaS32r

figure 86 Unknown Author. 📱. Pinterest, 2021. https://www.pinterest.ca/pin/884464814290430510/

figure 87 Gab Bois. Photograph Phoney Heels. GabBois, 2021. http://www.gabbois.com/

figure 88 John Yuyi. Shoe Laces Charger. Cargo Collective, April, 2016. https://cargocollective.com/johnyuyi/shoe-laces-charger

figure 89 Unknown Author. Green Slippers. Cloudfront. Year Unknown.https://d2w9rnfcy7mm78.cloudfront.net/214935/original_7189aaf6a0714cd927c46a9de-6c0e29b.jpg?1394678903?bc=1

figure 90 Vick Cammie. O ano é 2007...... Você tá no recreio com seus amigos, usando um fonezinho, ouvindo uma musiquinha... O que tá tocando? No meu até hoje Last Night do P Diddy. Instagram. December, 2019. https://www.instagram.com/p/B5scN6jneDy/

figure 91 Michiko Matsushita. Nails, 1999. Instagram. August, 2017. https://www.instagram.com/p/BX5hynSIB-NM/?taken-by=another___kind

figure 92 bellafleurz. eurotrashbaby. Tumbig. 2022. https://www.tumbig.com/blog/eurotrashbaby

figure 93 Gab Bois. Photograph Sound On. GabBois, 2017. http://www.gabbois.com/

figure 94 The Tech Gets. Facebook Would Like to Access Your Heart Rate. Tumblr, 2018. https://thetechgets.tumblr.com/post/172243957495/seriously-seems-like-they-need-all-kind-of-info

figure 95 Morgan Sutherland. Girl With The Headphones. Arena, 2016. https://d2w9rnfcy7mm78.cloudfront.net/629110/original_a9851f48f0764b4067ad27d1a6c-2c6da.jpg?1465195141?bc=1

figure 96 Cyborg Arts Limited. Photograph of Neil Harbisson. Cyborg Arts, 2020. https://www.cyborgarts.com/neil-harbisson

figure 97 Sondra Perry. Video, combined computer-based media, and performance in Young Women Sitting and Standing And Talking and Stuff, 2021. https://dotconnectorstudio.com/portfolio/tech-as-art/

figure 98 Author unknown. Synergy Tek. January, 2020. https://synergytek.com.tw/blog/tag/遠距醫療

figure 99 Jason Urgo, 2012. Screenshot from The Operation - Eye Witness Laser Eye Surgery Day 1a. YouTube. https://www.youtube.com/watch?v=LDNry3DnrhA&t=1s

figure 100 PreScouter. Quantified Self. PreScouter, August 2013. https://www.prescouter.com/2013/08/can-the-quantified-self-be-your-competitive-advantage/quantifiedself/

figure 101 Yirui Xue et al. Commercial and Scientific Solutions for Blood Glucose Monitoring—A Review. MDPI. January, 2022. https://www.mdpi.com/1424-8220/22/2/425

figure 102 GenMice. Photograph of Crown Prince Of Dubai Sheik Hamdan bin Mohammed Al Maktoum. GenMice, January 2021. https://genmice.com/unknown-facts/This-Prince-Of-Dubai-Owns-Some-Of-The-Rarest-And-Costliest-T/

figure 103 Expert Vagabond. Top Smartphone Cameras For Traveling. Expertvagabond, January 2022. https://expertvagabond.com/best-travel-camera/

figure 104 NeRF-W technology. 3D Rendering of Trevi Fountain from Thousands of Tourist Photos. Google, 2020. https://nerf-w.github.io/

figure 105 Author Unknown. Crowd at Mona Lisa. Keep-CalmAndWander, 2018. https://www.keepcalmandwander.com/monalisa-at-louvre-museum-paris-france/

figure 106 Azul Inho. Tourists Go Home. Twitter, july 2021. https://mobile.twitter.com/_azulinho/status/1418915782432641040

figure 107 Katie Wang. Tourist with selfie stick. ANACA-PRI, ITALY, 2015. https://www.nationalgeographic.com/travel/article/photo-contest-spontaneous-moments

figure 108 Author Unknown. Making picture of Mona Lisa. Cleanmemes, 2016. https://cleanmemes.com/category/clean-funny-images/page/170/

figure 109 Gerhard Haderer. Sunset. Keblog. Year unknown. https://www.keblog.it/illustrazioni-satiriche-societa-gerhard-haderer/

figure 110 Phillip. TIPS FOR TAKING PERFECT FOOD PHOTOS USING YOUR PHONE. SouthernFATTY.com, 2017. https://www.southernfatty.com/food-photos-with-phone/

figure 111 Image With No Author. Storage upgrade of brain. NEJM Knowledge+, May 2015. https://knowledge-plus.nejm.org/blog/learning-and-memory/

figure 112 Tese Jurdica. Confira 8 excelentes dicas para você aprimorar sua memória. TeseJurdica, September 2016. https://tesejuridica.com.br/confira-8-excelentes-dicas-para-voce-aprimorar-sua-memoria/

figure 113 Gray Crawford. Four months of conversation. Twitter, 2021. https://twitter.com/graycrawford/status/1400884788718825474

figure 114 Fredrik Solli Wandem. Smartphone in concert. Unplash, 2019. https://unsplash.com/photos/E0y-v6DR3j_w

figure 115 Peter Kennard. Photomontage of Tony Blair taking a selfie in front of a huge explosion. Photo Op, 2007. https://www.iwm.org.uk/collections/item/object/42971#:~:text=kennardphillipps%2C%20Photo%20Op%20(2007),known%20images%20of%20that%20period.

figure 116 Lindsey Albin. 200 Photos In May. PDF, 2021.

figure 117 Author Unknown. Selfies from Below. Tumblr. Year unknown. https://selfiesfrombelow.tumblr.com

figure 118 Author Unknown. Selfies from Below. Tumblr. Year unknown. https://selfiesfrombelow.tumblr.com

figure 119 Author Unknown. Selfies from Below. Tumblr. Year unknown. https://selfiesfrombelow.tumblr.com

figure 120 Author Unknown. Selfies from Below. Tumblr. Year unknown. https://selfiesfrombelow.tumblr.com

figure 121 Author Unknown. Selfies from Below. Tumblr. Year unknown. https://selfiesfrombelow.tumblr.com

figure 122 Ieva Jakusa. Double chin of Ernest. 2022. Orginal work.

figure 123 Author Unknown. Selfies from Below. Tumblr. Year unknown. https://selfiesfrombelow.tumblr.com

figure 124 Johan Deckmann. Book installation Censor Yourself. Instagram, 2021. https://www.instagram.com/p/CZW8TNysR9V/

figure 125 Adrien Picard. DOn2A_cXkAE2E_6.jpg Are.na, 2018. https://www.are.na/block/1552462

figure 126 Piketchup. Recycle Bin. Reddit, R/softwaregore, 2019. https://www.reddit.com/r/softwaregore/comments/av1fhc/recycle_bin/?utm_source=share&utm_medium=web2x&context=3

figure 127 Ieva Jakusa. This story is no longer available. Instagram, 2022.

figure 128 Ieva Jakusa. Deleted msg. WhatsApp, 2022.

figure 129 Alessandro Bianchi / Reuters. Priests take pictures as Pope Francis arrives to lead a mass at the Los Samanes park in Guayaquil, Ecuador. Buzzfeed, July 2015. https://www.buzzfeed.com/gabrielsanchez/the-most-powerful-photos-of-this-week-july-10

figure 130 MVMedia. Phone in Mosque. Muslim Village, March 2017. https://muslimvillage.com/2017/03/03/122552/screen-invades-masjid/

figure 131 Author Unknown. Photograph Pope Francis blesses the child's image through his mobile phone. Sala Nervi at the Christian Workers Movement, January 16, 2016. https://www.dailymail.co.uk/news/article-3402562/Pope-Francis-takes-time-busy-schedule-bless-lady-s-photograph-young-child-phone.html

figure 132 Image With No Author. Phys, August 2017. https://phys.org/news/2017-08-smartphone-age-hajj.html

figure 133 Andreas Solaro. Pope Francis speaks on the phone during his weekly general audience at Paul VI hall in the Vatican, on August 11, 2021. https://www.timesofisrael.com/liveblog_entry/israeli-rabbis-send-letter-to-vatican-expressing-concern-over-papal-remarks/

figure 134 Image With No Author. Year Unknown.

figure 135 Arena Commons. Baby sleeping. Arena, 2019. https://www.are.na/block/4283278

figure 136 Mitchel Cox. 51d4b6722c1f25fc-c83770097e6529b9.jpg Arena, 2018. https://i.pinimg.com/originals/51/d4/b6/51d4b6722c1f25fc-c83770097e6529b9.jpg

figure 137 MikaMax. Lazy Neck Smartphone Houder. https://www.bol.com/nl/nl/p/mikamax-lazy-neck-smart-phone-houder-telefoonhouder-gsm-houder-telefoon-standaard-handsfree-te-gebruiken-als-selfie-stick-ver-stelbaar-universeel-55-cm/9200000130019810/?Re-ferrer=ADVNLGOO002015-G-139200340315-S-1678965972374-9200000130019810&g-clid=Cj0KCQjw8uOWBhDXARIsAOxKJ2GG-wrrkR3KgQYgpTm0p25TJEMmuAgnIAOkpfDE11SxuGF-sUtd7C3osaAu_IEALw_wcB

figure 138 TollFreeForwarding. 3D model Mindy. Toll-FreeForwarding, 2019. https://www.digit.fyi/how-will-technology-change-the-human-body-by-2100/

figure 139 Author unknown. მოხერხებულია. Inter-media. 2021. https://intermedia.ge/სურათი/634565-მოხერხებულია/187/

figure 140 Delta Technology. iArm Forearm Mount. Geeky Gadgets, September 2010. https://www.geeky-gadgets.com/iarm-forearm-mount-humour-29-09-2010/

figure 141 Ungrip. B*tch-slapped by a phone. Kickstarter, 2017. https://www.kickstarter.com/projects/ungripyour-phone/ungrip-hold-your-phone-in-comfort-style-and-many-w?lang=zh

figure 142 Otago Daily Times. Screenshot from Wish. September 2020. https://www.odt.co.nz/star-news/star-national/down-drain-phones-showers-scupper-ing-sustainability

figure 143 Jupitaire. Screenshot from Keeping Up With The Kardashians. Tumblr. https://jupitaire.tumblr.com

figure 144 Author unknown. Arena. 2020. https://www.are.na/block/7306276

figure 145 Stickerlight. Using my 17" Macbook while float-ing in the Dead Sea in Israel. Reddit. 2013. https://www.reddit.com/r/pics/comments/1etork/using_my_17_mac-book_while_floating_in_the_dead/

figure 146 João Pedro Rodrigues. Morning of Saint Antho-ny's Day. MUBI, 2012. https://mubi.com/films/morning-of-saint-anthonys-day

figure 147 Thijs Jaeger. alt14.png Arena, 2019. https://d2w9rnfcy7mm78.cloudfront.net/3860335/original_c3312083ab102ef6b33cb3cb8cf25989.png?1552559833?bc=1

figure 148 Ieva Jakusa. Txt meme. 2022. Original work.

figure 149 Dexta Robotics. Dexmo F2 Glove Prototype. Diversus. December, 2016. https://www.diversus.com.au/en/Our-News/2016-12-Augmented-and-Virtual-Reality---Where-is-it-going

figure 150 どらすと. Screenshot from ZZ Gundam. Twitter. December, 2019. https://twitter.com/mobile_sheet/sta-tus/1203670942372651008

figure 151 YouBionic. Augmented Human. Youtube. No-vember, 2017. https://www.youtube.com/watch?v=O4ng-PRSuyO0

figure 152 BROADBANDCHOICES. An illustration of what our hands might look like if they evolved for cellphone use. Broadbandchoices, 2017.https://eu.indystar.com/story/news/2017/10/05/see-how-gnarly-your-hands-would-look-like-if-they-evolved-smartphone-use/735365001/

figure 153 Eni Farhani Binti Abu Malek. U.S. National Texting Championship. Public Relations Peeps, April 2012. http://publicrelationspeeps.blogspot.com/2012/04/raising-awareness-for-new-text.html

figure 154 The Master. Safe Internet!. Funny Junk. https://funnyjunk.com/funny_pictures/1850360/Safe/

figure 155 The Meta Picture. Decode Your Teen Txt Lin-go!. Daft. December, 2013. https://content.daft.io/nowo/text-message-nightmares-1191073-Dec2013/

figure 156 Sandika. Mobile Phone Jail Cell. Amazon. https://www.amazon.ca/Smartphone-Holders-Class-room-Storage-Family/dp/B07M9W1WM1?th=1

figure 157 Yatú. Trust This Person? Arena. 2020. https://www.are.na/block/8173326

figure 158 Sandika. Mobile Phone Jail Cell. Amazon. https://www.amazon.ca/Smartphone-Holders-Class-room-Storage-Family/dp/B07M9W1WM1?th=1

figure 159 Dokkiri. Hand iPhone Case. John Rieber. February, 2014. https://johnrieber.com/2014/02/13/a-japanese-hand-i-phone-the-craziest-i-phone-cover-ever-handy-too/

figure 160 HiComm. December, 2017. https://hicomm.bg/lubopitno/nad-1000-prilozheniya-za-android-i-ios-izpolz-vat-softuer-koito-zapisvat-vseki-zvuk-okolo-nas.html

figure 161 TrinityP3. September, 2015. https://www.trinityp3.com/2015/09/digital-data-technology-advice/

figure 162 Justin Crowe And Aric Snee. Selfie Arm. April, 2015. https://www.wired.co.uk/article/selfie-stick-arm

figure 163 Tom Sibma. Arena. 2021. https://www.are.na/block/9751819

figure 164 Twitpic. Dog Selfie. Insider. January, 2014. https://www.businessinsider.com/photos-from-the-self-ie-olympics-2014-1?international=true&r=US&IR=T

figure 165 Macaque Selfie. Bored Panda. 2017. https://www.boredpanda.com/funny-animal-selfies/?utm_source=google&utm_medium=organic&utm_campaign=or-ganic

figure 166 KrozMDC. Cat takes selfie to prove he is being abused. Imgur. October, 2014. https://imgur.com/7H-GNSvA

figure 167 Yoremahm. Manny The Selfie Cat. Instagram. January, 2017. https://www.instagram.com/p/BP-TUqu0DLkS/?taken-by=yoremahm

figure 168 Pablo Rochat. Image Alarm. Instagram, 2019. https://www.instagram.com/p/CTUI2QALrnrd/

figure 169 Image With No Author. Year unknown.

figure 170 Image With No Author. Quick reactions. Insta-gram, Year unknown.

figure 171 Pablo Rochat. 🌍. 2020, Instagram. https://www.instagram.com/p/CEW1ybYhmOa/

figure 172 Pablo Rochat. Image !. Instagram, 2020.

figure 173 Anastasia Davydova Lewis. 78E901DF-9D5C-4B5E-8A13-3237A77C246C.jpg Arena, 2017. https://www.are.na/block/1130625

figure 174 Khamosh Pathak. Emoji Reactions in Instagram DMs. How To Geek, December 2020. https://www.howtogeek.com/698109/how-to-change-emoji-reactions-in-instagram-dms/

figure 175 u/the_swedish_cow. Cyberpunk 2077. Reddit, 2020. https://www.reddit.com/r/memes/comments/hpwp77/cyberpunk_2077/

figure 176-178 Marcello Gómez Maureira. Tender - It's how people meat. Vimeo, 2015. https://www.vice.com/en/article/yp5bew/this-piece-of-meat-just-swiped-right

figure 179 Elliott Cost. Life Online. Arena, 2020. https://image.elliott.computer/pocket-keyboard-1.jpg

figure 180 lotalota_. Girl Reading. Instagram story, 2022.

figure 181 Image With no Author. Task Force Arrests 500 Illegal Miners In Ondo. Independent Newspaper Nigeria. June, 2020. https://independent.ng/task-force-arrests-500-illegal-miners-in-ondo/

figure 182 Ajour Mag. December, 2019. https://www.ajourmag.ch/billionen-des-schreckens2/

figure 183 Ulet Ifansasti. Image from series Friends of the Earth. Belo Laut village, 2013. https://www.theguardian.com/environment/2013/jul/12/apple-tin-mining-bangka-island-iphone

figure 184 Steve Jobs holding iPhone 1, 2007. 9 to 5 Mac. April, 2022. https://9to5mac.com/2022/04/13/facebook-ar-glasses-iphone-moment/

figure 185 Ulet Ifansasti. Image from series Friends of the Earth. Belo Laut village, 2013. https://www.theguardian.com/environment/2013/jul/12/apple-tin-mining-bangka-island-iphone

figure 186 Matthew Hattingh. An African dream made real with SA's first smartphone factory. News24, 2019. https://www.news24.com/citypress/business/an-african-dream-made-real-with-sas-first-smartphone-factory-20191104

figure 187 Reuters/KCNA. Photo Of Kim Jong Un Inspecting North Korea's First Smartphone Factory. Business Insider. August, 2013. https://www.businessinsider.com/kim-jong-un-north-korea-smartphone-factory-2013-8?international=true&r=US&IR=T

figure 188 Xiaomi. Xiaomi Will Open Stores and Manufacture Phones in Argentina. Android Republic. February, 2022. https://androidrepublic.tech/xiaomi-will-open-stores-and-manufacture-phones-in-argentina/

figure 189 Garry Ing. liang-ban-stutter. Arena, 2020. https://d2w9rnfcy7mm78.cloudfront.net/8979682/original_4459b7fbb3d46463724ddc2488c0f7ac.jpg?1601903871?bc=0

figure 190 FishySmellz. Taxi dashboard. Hong Kong, 2017. https://www.reddit.com/r/WTF/comments/7feek3/the_dashboard_in_the_cab_i_took_today_in_hong/

figure 191 u/jkevintu. Pokémon GO. Reddit, 2019. https://www.reddit.com/r/pics/comments/d5c3o4/the_pok%C3%A9mon_go_grandpa_now_has_45_phones_on_his/

figure 192 Jim Urquhart/Reuters/Newscom. Burning Man. Esquire. September, 2017. https://www.esquire.com/lifestyle/news/g3562/best-burning-man-photos-2017/?slide=4

figure 193 Simon Weckert. Performance and Installation Google Maps Hacks. Berlin, 2020. http://www.simon-weckert.com/googlemapshacks.html

figure 194 American Artist. No State. Zuccaire Gallery. 2018. https://zuccairegallery.stonybrook.edu/exhibitions/_past/iconicity_2019.php

figure 195 Terkel Gjervig. Arena. 2019. https://www.are.na/block/3001505

figure 196 OK-RM and Matthieu Lavanchy. Home Economics #13. Venice Architecture Biennale, 2016. Wallpaper*. May, 2016. https://www.wallpaper.com/architecture/2016-venice-architecture-biennale-british-pavilion-curators-take-us-on-a-tour-of-the-modern-home

figure 197 Image with No Author. Twitter. August, 2016. https://twitter.com/bu4a_13/status/766838298300059648

figure 198 İsmail Enes Ayhan.Electric Control Cabinet Production Factory, Kayseri, Türkiye. Unsplash. March, 2020. https://unsplash.com/photos/lVZjvw-u9V8

figure 199 Scarlett Entertainment. Phone Charging Stations. https://scarlettentertainment.com/acts/event-phone-chargers

figure 200 Lucas de Ruiter. Project Bathing in the Cloud - Computational Fluid Dynamics. Design Academy Eindhoven 2020.

figure 201 Jesse Kanda. Image Firefly. Jesse Kanda, 2014. http://www.jessekanda.com

figure 202 Kidmograph. Human Electromagnetism. Human Frequencies. Year unknown. https://www.human-frequencies.com

figure 203 Dave Dildine/WTOP. Flash floods strike Washington, DC, area during busy commute. ABC News. July, 2019. https://abcnews.go.com/US/severe-storms-expected-rockies-midwest/story?id=64186871

figure 204 Yash Reddy. Shees Park - Fujairah - United Arab Emirates. Unplash, 2021. https://unsplash.com/photos/5SZGMU_KRec

figure 205 Awesome Stuff. This Man Fights Against the Strong Winds- Man Vs Nature | Hurricane Irma #Hurricane-Florence US. Youtube. September, 2017. https://www.youtube.com/watch?v=IB-QujSzpBY

figure 206 Image With no Author. AK-47 Selfie Stick. Imgur. 2015. https://imgur.com/gallery/LGELUIW/comment/419050671

figure 207 Author unknown. Twitter. December, 2020. https://twitter.com/ivanwyaa/status/1339069913667866624

figure 208 Image with no Author. Selfie While Flying A Plane. Year Unknown. https://www.egwtrade.com/?product_id=284845345_47

figure 209 Author unknown. Hello moto. Arena. January, 2021. https://www.are.na/block/10411080

figure 210 Splitpics. Apple Trees. The Sun. March, 2018. https://www.thesun.ie/fabulous/2344680/the-rich-kids-of-instagram-show-off-their-problems-from-using-bank-notes-as-loo-roll-to-pouring-champagne-down-the-drain/

figure 211 Image With No Author. Alcachondeo. 2018. https://alcachondeo.net/las-imagenes-mas-chistosas-de-la-red/

figure 212 Teresa Fernande Zpello. Candleholder Post-tech flame. teresafernandezpello, 2020. https://teresafernandezpello.com/Post-tech-flame

figure 213 Arthur Röing Baer. 068.JPG Are.na, 2017. https://d2w9rnfcy7mm78.cloudfront.net/1018166/original_cb427fdcb25ac9577fc9dfe844efea78.jpg?1494587926?bc=1

figure 214 Neurocam. Youtube. October, 2013. https://www.youtube.com/watch?v=W67LvAYAkY4

figure 215 Alexis O'Hara. Squeeeque. Everyday Lis-

tening. 2010. http://www.everydaylistening.com/articles/2010/10/1/more-todaysart-2010.html
figure 216 geoffreyk55. Gaming, Technology. Images, 2017. https://www.myconfinedspace.com/2017/07/17/the-future-of-vr-gaming/
figure 217 Image With No Author. Year unknown.
figure 218 Amasty. Screenshot Terms and Conditions. Year unknown. https://amasty.com/docs/doku.php?id=magento_1:gdpr
figure 219 Wired. Meme of Mark Zuckerberg at the Congress. Wired Italia. April, 2018. https://www.wired.it/galleries/gait85667/
figure 220 Image With No Author. Year unknown.
figure 221 Image With No Author. Year unknown.
figure 222 iCulture. Face ID: Tweede gezicht instellen of een ander uiterlijk. December, 2020. https://www.iculture.nl/tips/face-id-tweede-gezicht/
figure 223 Nokia Fossile. Meme. Year Unknown. https://me.me/i/naokia-nokia-fossil-d984b057e71d-4b8780a1d9dd3c14b9da
figure 224 Apple. Phone Prototype, 1983. Mashable. 2011. https://mashable.com/archive/apple-iphone-1983
figure 225 Steffanie Padilla. Image Arrow. Are.na, 2020. https://d2w9rnfcy7mm78.cloudfront.net/6713467/original_1169ef1dc8cf77f4884aba4089fa346e.png?1585952457?bc=0
figure 226 IBM. Personal Communicator Simon. IBM, 1992. https://www.troyhistoricvillage.org/december-16-smartphones/
figure 227 Zack Dougherty. Twitter profile picture. Twitter. https://twitter.com/zackdougherty
figure 228 whiteferrariboys. Instagram. October, 2021. https://www.instagram.com/p/CVdzGg1IbM4/
figure 229 Fi. Arena. 2021. https://www.are.na/block/9550427
figure 230 Mathieu Denis. obsolete 3. Instagram, 2021. https://www.instagram.com/p/CWIIV8tjNLm/
figure 231 Shujaa Aman. 11 Reasons to Start Using Apple Pay. Make Use Of. June, 2022. https://www.makeuseof.com/reasons-to-start-using-apple-pay/
figure 232 Urdiales Andruw, 2020. All Evil. Digital Scan. Are.na https://d2w9rnfcy7mm78.cloudfront.net/5731749/original_bc0e23e8c9877f5e1a43f7a7595d5115.jpg?1576527655?bc=0
figure 233 Meme. Payment options iPhone 11. Year and source unknown.
figure 234 Demotywatory. Glos Wielkopolski. Year unknown. https://gloswielkopolski.pl/zus-internauci-nas-miewaja-sie-z-zakladu-ubezpieczen-spolecznych-memy/ga/c15-13503089/zd/31224687
figure 235 TVPWorld. Pay-eye: Your money's gone in the blink of an eye. TVP World. November, 2020. https://tvpworld.com/50603127/payeye-your-moneys-gone-in-the-blink-of-an-eye
figure 236 Steph Davidson. Illustration. Bloomberg. March, 2013. https://www.bloomberg.com/news/articles/2013-03-28/bitcoin-may-be-the-global-economys-last-safe-haven#xj4y7vzkg
figure 237 Barack Obama Presidential Library. President Barack Obama. June, 2014. https://www.obamalibrary.gov/photos-videos
figure 238 Ieva Jakusa. Keep Browsing Data, 2022. Original Work.
figure 239 Author Unknown. I'm Gonna Live on After I Die. Tumblr. https://78.media.tumblr.com/

d7a835305a0842a89eb2662aeb07e551/tumblr_nfr74h-bgSM1r1qx4so4_500.jpg
figure 240 Laura Rivera. Broken electronic personal device. Unsplash, 2020. https://unsplash.com/photos/3a7SyW0h8vQ
figure 241 Nelson Aguilar. Screenshot iPhone. Gadget Hacks. 2020. https://ios.gadgethacks.com/how-to/use-trick-quickly-select-all-photos-videos-your-iphone-bulk-delete-share-0312925/
figure 242 u/Mo0oG. Wiring tunnel inside an abandoned coal power plant. Reddit, 2017. https://www.reddit.com/r/cableporn/comments/64katk/wiring_tunnel_inside_an_abandoned_coal_power_plant/
figure 243 David Parkins. The World's Most Valuable Resource. The Economist. May, 2017. https://www.economist.com/leaders/2017/05/06/the-worlds-most-valuable-resource-is-no-longer-oil-but-data
figure 244 Copier Coller, Steven Mazzola, Igo Studio, Coline Munier. Arena. 2019. https://www.are.na/block/3332277
figure 245 Unknown Author. Boys with connected headphones. Pikabu. 2018. https://pikabu.ru/story/skovannyie_odnoy_tsepyu_svyazannyie_odnoy_tselyu_5848241
figure 246 Barrett Lyon. Opte Project. Opte, 2005. https://www.opte.org/the-internet
figure 247 David Avazzadeh. 1nfluencing. Humble Arts Foundation Group Show #59. Hafny. http://hafny.org/group-show-59-numerology
figure 248 Unknown Author. Nokia hands. Source unknown.
figure 249 Author Unknown. Chat With A Live Person. Year unknown.
figure 250 Benjamin Edwards. The Wacky World of VR in the 80s and 90s. PCMAG. April 2018. www.pcmag.com/news/the-wacky-world-of-vr-in-the-80s-and-90s
figure 251 Unknown Author. Anime characters using flip phones. Kita Saling Belajar. August, 2014. http://kita-saling-belajar.blogspot.com/2014/08/dasar-dasar-komunikasi-part-2.html
figure 252 Kunxo. Flip Phone single artwork. Soundcloud. 2019. https://soundcloud.com/yungkkun/flip-phone
figure 253 nn
figure 254 Unknown Author. Anime characters using iPhone. Where Does The Anime Leave Off? March, 2021. https://wheredoestheanimeleaveoff.com/where-does-the-noragami-anime-leave-off-in-the-manga/
figure 255 Author Unknown. Anime flip phone. INF News. July, 2022. https://inf.news/en/digital/98107b1ad28632d0f66badbe1c1e41cf.html
figure 256 Unknown Author. So Much Internet, So Little Time. Cosmique Studio. Year unknown. https://cosmique-studio.com/so-little-time-tee/
figure 257 Pablo Rochat. 🐸. Instagram, 2019. https://www.instagram.com/p/Bveu2vGBOCN/?hl=en
figure 258 Kyliën Bergh. efada569f-7da2549e545e9151130e117.jpg. Arena, 2020. https://d2w9rnfcy7mm78.cloudfront.net/7599909/original_2ae551080cf5a8356200846d023fc3f0.jpg?1591699846?bc=0
figure 259 Unknown Author.The only way out is in. Unknown Year.
figure 260 Garry Ing. us06922815-20050726-d00000.png. Arena, 2018. https://www.are.na/block/2682743
figure 261 Vala Afshar. Updated Maslow's hierarchy of needs. Twitter, 2014. https://twitter.com/valaafshar/sta-

tus/51562150481471078?lang=en
figure 262 pranavmistry. All these open windows, but no fresh air. Twitter, 2014. https://twitter.com/pranavmistry/status/525540636607250432?lang=en
figure 263 Unknown Author. ◯👎. Facebook. December, 2021. https://www.facebook.com/confortablez/photos/a.2068946006496555/4908574945866966
figure 264 Mateusz Lengling. Cover Arts. Design Collector. 2017. https://designcollector.xyz/likes/cover-arts-by-mateusz-lengling
figure 265 Josh Kline. Skittles. MoMA, 2014. https://www.moma.org/collection/works/192069
figure 266 Sebastian Campion. Urban Cursor. Medium. October, 2015. https://medium.com/after-us/navigating-neoliberalism-f9fae2405488
figure 267 Андрей Разборов. Emoji roadblock. Carsguru. 2019. https://carsguru.net/news/36531/view.html
figure 268 Twitpic. Photos From The Selfie Olympics. Business Insider. January, 2014. https://www.businessinsider.com/photos-from-the-selfie-olympics-2014-1?international=true&r=US&IR=T
figure 269 Tyrone Stewart. Civilisations AR. Mobile Marketing Magazine. February, 2018. https://mobilemarketingmagazine.com/bbc-civilisations-ar-app
figure 270 Nicole Nguyen. Pokemon Go, augmented reality mode. Buzzfeed. December, 2017. https://www.buzzfeednews.com/article/nicolenguyen/how-new-pokemon-go-iphone-ar-mode-works
figure 271 Virtue. The Last Statement T-shirt. Carlings, 2019. https://www.highsnobiety.com/p/carlings-the-last-statement-t-shirt/
figure 272 WANNA. Explore new sneakers in AR! Youtube. January, 2019. https://www.youtube.com/watch?v=UmJriqzDUTo
figure 273 Cuseum. Museum From Home. AppStore, 2020. https://cuseum.com/ar-museum-from-home
figure 274 Adam Pickard. IKEA augmented-reality app. Dezeen, 2018. https://www.dezeen.com/2018/03/23/ikea-assembly-made-easier-through-augmented-reality-app/
figure 275 Author Unknown. Google is GOD. Imgflip. 2020. https://imgflip.com/memetemplate/237958325/Google-is-GOD
figure 276 Author Unknown. Spiritual computing. DIS Magazine. Year unknown. http://dismagazine.com/discussion/6770/dis-dump-fm/
figure 277 Aleksandra Belinskaya/Shutterstock. Meditation app. Shape. December, 2021. https://www.shape.com/lifestyle/mind-and-body/best-meditation-apps-beginners#89c7bab0-ce8d-4710-bbca-8576f73604b9
figure 278 Author Unknown. Phone parrot tongues GIF. GIFER. Year unknown. https://gifer.com/en/Bfev
figure 279 Fred Rogers. Sparrows talking about the future of the web. Arena. 2018. https://www.are.na/block/2178263
figure 280 Animal World. Baby dove want's to use cell phone / bird playing with cell phone. YouTube, 2020. https://www.youtube.com/watch?v=vYHRaVBYe-8I&list=PLHrQcnly9KpasTtC2d6xV7KSKYSDb4wV1
figure 281 Oskar Radon. Emoji. Arena. 2020. https://www.are.na/block/6334025
figure 282 Mary von Aue. Modern discourse. Twitter. February, 2017. https://twitter.com/von_owie/status/836656730079641601
figure 283 David Rodrigues et al. Lisbon Emoji and Emot-

icon Database (LEED): Norms for emoji and emoticons in nine evaluative dimensions. Springer. March, 2017. https://link.springer.com/content/pdf/10.3758%2Fs13428-017-0878-6.pdf
figure 284 & walsh. Emoji pack design. Instagram, 2020. https://www.instagram.com/p/B_UhQargEgK/?igshid=1vh8xntwahhdh
figure 285 Simon Evans. Vocabulary. New York, 2011. https://www.jamescohan.com/exhibitions/simon-evans2/selected-works?view=slider#10
figure 286 Oskar Radon. Emoji. Arena. 2020. https://www.are.na/block/7753698
figure 287 Benjamin Chaykin. Emoji Center. Vimeo, 2017. https://vimeo.com/195768959?embedded=true&source=video_title&owner=765757
figure 288 Associated Press. Large mobile phone. Business Insider. June, 2011. https://www.businessinsider.com/future-of-mobile-2011-6?international=true&r=US&IR=T
figure 289 Olaf Speier. Brick phone stock image. Dreamstime. Year unknown. https://www.dreamstime.com/stock-photo-brick-phone-guy-using-large-simualating-big-smartphone-funny-technology-concept-image87908010
figure 290 Author Unknown. Large Apple Airpod. Pinterest. Year unknown. https://nl.pinterest.com/pin/791051122044454865/
figure 291 Simon Abranowicz. Brick Phone. 2020. https://simon.abranowicz.com/#project-gq.com
figure 292 Jiuta. Tumblr. Year unknown. https://pompompurin.tumblr.com/post/644112648007450624
figure 293 Katritikkanen. MCbling. Gifer. 2017. https://gifer.com/en/74Iu
figure 294 Dimas Djay. iPhone Altar. Medium. July, 2017. https://medium.com/@orepras/meme-marketing-bi-ar-ngetren-972d0feb2f0
figure 295 Ma Nu. Paris Hilton with phone. Arena. July, 2022. https://www.are.na/block/16642075
figure 296 Author Unknown. phone flash! Kera Magazine, 2001. https://www.tumbig.com/tag/cyber-style
figure 297 lanetechdiamond. Cellphone Tombstone. Lane Tech Diamond. January, 2016. https://lanetechdiamond.org/cellphone-tombstone/
figure 298 Author Unknown. Crying Tombstone. Year Unknown.
figure 299 Author Unknow. Creative Tombstones. EBaumsWorld, 2015. https://www.ebaumsworld.com/pictures/creative-tombstones/84647990/
figure 300 ssouthsides. Headstone in shape of iPhone. New Zealand, 2019. https://www.tiktok.com/@ssouthsides/video/7086596871916915970
figure 301 Author Unknown. iPhone headstone. AppleInsider. September, 2018. https://appleinsider.com/articles/18/09/28/woman-immortalized-by-5-foot-iphone-headstone-in-russia
figure 302 Author Unknown. Thank You For Engaging with my Content. Arena. 2019. https://www.are.na/block/2965583

SWIPE
Smartphone movie

www.nextnature.net/swipe

COLOPHON

CONCEPT & AUTHOR
Mieke Gerritzen

**RESEARCH &
IMAGE SELECTION**
Ieva Jakusa

DESIGN
Ieva Jakusa
Mieke Gerritzen

GLOSSARY
Beau Magdelijns

EDITOR
Ruben Baart

PRODUCER
Next Nature
www.nextnature.net

PRINTHOUSE
Real Concepts, Velp

FONTS
Helvetica Neue
MIU MIU

PAPER
Munken Pure 120g

MANY THANKS TO
Hans Maarten van den Brink
Iris van Hest
Geert Lovink
Koert van Mensvoort

ISBN 978-90-636965-7-3

This publication has generously been supported by